5 PLUS 5

5 INGREDIENTS + 5 MINUTES PREP!

Deliciously Easy Recipes from your Rice Cooker

Deb Roussou

Pascoe Publishing, Inc.
Rocklin, California

Acknowledgements – Our heartfelt thanks and appreciation go to Todd Rogers and Kyle Erickson at Aroma® Housewares Company. Without their visionary concepts and technical edits, this book would be far less informative and certainly not as fun. We never knew Spam™ could be so good – thanks, guys!

Cover & Interior Design by KB Designs
Published in the United States of America by

Pascoe Publishing, Inc.
Rocklin, California
www.pascoepublishing.com

ISBN: 978-1-929862-85-6

14

10   9   8   7   6   5   4   3

Printed in China

table of contents

introduction

If ever there was a kitchen appliance made to make your life easier and mealtime more relaxing, it's your rice cooker. Oh, sure, you've heard these general claims before. But, really. Check out the fact that there are 125 recipes in this cookbook containing 5, FIVE, ingredients or less, all of which create amazingly delicious dishes. Think about that. Imagine shopping for a week's worth of dinners – a different dinner each night, by the way – and getting only 5 ingredients for each. Now, you're seeing what we're saying.

Your rice cooker prepares rice beautifully, and that's probably why you bought it in the first place, but in the course of writing this cookbook, we also found that a lovely variety of foods can be quickly and easily assembled into one-dish meals, desserts, side dishes, breads and breakfasts – using 5 ingredients and 5 minutes prep time or less. And, one of the most inviting features, the Steam/Cook function, allows you to sauté at a higher heat before proceeding with your recipe prep. This eliminates the hassle of using another pan or adding another step to the recipes you prepare. In the end, you'll have only one pot to clean and that's the way a smart cook likes to finish every meal. Bottom line: we're talking about more time to relax, less stress running through the grocery store and some pretty amazing dishes coming from this champ of a rice cooker.

On to some explanations: In creating these recipes, the assumption has been made that you already have a few staples – basic food items – on hand. For example, you should have white flour, white and brown sugar, oil, butter and salt and pepper in your pantry. If you don't have items such as salt and pepper, you might want to make one big shopping run to pick up staple items before getting started. Also, you should have toothpicks in order to prepare some of the appetizer recipes. Even if you don't use toothpicks while cooking, they come in handy for science projects, so get some anyway.

Each recipe will designate which items are considered "have on hand" essentials and other items that count toward the "5" ingredients. Here is a general list of what we consider basic food items:

Milk	Mayonnaise	Lemon Pepper	Baking Powder
Butter	Cooking Spray	Water	White Sugar
Extra-virgin Olive Oil	Salt	Soy Sauce	Brown Sugar
Canola Oil	Black Pepper	Flour (white)	

Notice that we haven't designated what kind of milk or whether or not you need salted or unsalted butter, margarine, etc. etc., and that's simply because why get into these details when you have enough to do already? Use what you have for all of these recipes and, if you need to make a little substitution here or there, so be it. If you don't have olive oil or canola oil, use regular vegetable oil instead – no big deal. Also, you may need to switch out quantities of some recipes, depending on what you have on hand. Mix and match to your heart's content, we say! The only exception to all of the above is if you try to use fake foods like artificial sugar or butter-substitute spray instead of real food, the end results might have to be fed to an unsuspecting pet.

For many of us, the dreaded walk through the grocery store at the end of the day is akin to walking the dog at midnight. There isn't much glamour in racing aisle to aisle through the store, throwing into your cart whatever items look vaguely familiar, as you contemplate doing it all over again tomorrow night. We're sympathetic to this plight because we've also walked that dog – we've given up on entirely too many recipes because we couldn't find fresh marjoram, arugula, frozen puff pastry, uncooked quinoa, or what have you. In the spirit of being good neighbors, we've included in several recipes here a call-out, titled "Where is it?" that will tell you what an ingredient is and then help you hunt it down in your own grocery store.

5 plus 5 secrets: When cooking with your rice cooker, remember those little lectures from your mom: wear oven mitts when placing food in or out of the hot inner pot; use a long-handled, heatproof plastic or wooden spoon for stirring (not the serving spatula); and be careful when handling hot liquids or hot foods in general. The inner pot gets really hot, so stir everything with carefree abandon and joy, but put on an oven mitt first.

About the Steam/Cook Feature: One of the nicest features of most rice cookers is that foods can be quickly sautéed and cooked in the inner pot using the Steam/Cook button. Many of the recipes in this book use this method, so here are some helpful hints:

» While Steam/Cook isn't specifically designed for sauteing, it reaches a high heat quickly to brown and sauté foods for a variety of recipes. Steam/Cook does have a built-in boil-dry protection, however, so once the temperature becomes too hot, it will switch over to Keep-Warm. If you need more time to sauté, just press the Steam/Cook button again.

» If you want to sauté or cook quickly without waiting for the cooker to warm up, preheat the empty inner pot for 5 minutes before placing any ingredients inside. Simply press the Steam/Cook button and wait until it shuts off. Add your ingredients to the inner pot (careful – it will be hot!) and sauté right away.

» Always use a long-handled wooden or plastic heat-resistant spoon when you are sauteing or stirring in your rice cooker. **Do not** use the serving spatula that came with your rice cooker. Any prep done at high heat calls for a sturdy long-handled spoon and a potholder or oven mitt. Play it smart!

Some of our yummy dessert recipes direct you to steam pudding or cake inside heatproof mugs. Pretty clever, actually. Just make sure your mugs are able to take the high heat for several minutes and will fit inside the inner pot. When done, lift the hot mugs out of the pot with extreme caution.

Finally, a word to every cook who truly cares and wants to do things right along the way. Take a deep breath now and then and slow down enough to enjoy meals together. Instead of dashing around and throwing the silverware on the table, or at each other, as attempted by our 2-year-old, add some graciousness to your life and take time for meals that contain one or two conversations, large or small. Leisurely conversations with those you love will always make the food taste better.

asparagus & swiss cheese omeletatta

HAVE ON HAND: 1 TBSP BUTTER, SALT & PEPPER | SERVES 4

Never heard of an "omeletatta?" Think of a melding between an omelet and a frittata – as in a yummy combo of tangy cheese and tender veggies within fluffy scrambled eggs. Yeah, now you're getting the picture. If you want to really impress your mother-in-law, cut the asparagus spears on the diagonal instead of straight across. That'll fix her.

4 thin spears fresh asparagus, cut into
    1-inch pieces
6 large eggs, beaten with a dash of salt and pepper
½ cup Swiss cheese, shredded
1 teaspoon fresh thyme leaves, chopped
1 green onion, chopped

Place the butter in the inner pot of the rice cooker and press the Steam/Cook button. Melt the butter and add the asparagus. Stir and sauté for about 4 minutes, stirring occasionally. Pour the eggs over the asparagus and scatter the remaining ingredients over the eggs. Close the lid and Steam/Cook for 12 to 14 minutes, or until the eggs are set. Slide the omeletatta onto a large serving plate, cut into large wedges and serve at once.

italian pesto omeletatta

HAVE ON HAND: 1 TBSP BUTTER, SALT & PEPPER | SERVES 4

A little pesto goes a long way, so go easy at first and then really break it out with two full tablespoons – or even a bit more – to send a big wake-up call at the table.

1 small shallot, peeled and chopped
1 small tomato, seeded and chopped
6 eggs, beaten with a dash of salt and pepper
½ cup Parmesan cheese, grated
2 tablespoons pesto sauce*

Place the butter in the inner pot of the rice cooker and press the Steam/Cook button. Melt the butter and add the shallots and tomato and sauté until softened. Toss in the remaining ingredients, season with salt and pepper to taste, and give it a quick stir. Close the lid and Steam/Cook for 12 to 14 minutes, or until the eggs are set. Use a serving spatula to slide the omeletatta onto a large serving plate. Cut into wedges and serve at once.

*WHERE IS IT? You can find pesto sauce in the refrigerator case at your grocery store, typically next to cartons of alfredo or marina sauce.

paul bunyan scramble

HAVE ON HAND: 1 TBSP BUTTER, SALT & PEPPER | SERVES 4

Hearty enough for a super-sized woodsman like Paul Bunyan and his blue ox, Babe, this country-style breakfast is so packed with flavor we guarantee a stampede of folks looking for more. So, what are you waiting for? Get to scramblin' those eggs.

½ lb. bulk country style pork sausage
2 cups pre-cooked frozen hash browns*, thawed
6 eggs, beaten with a dash of salt and pepper
2 green onions, chopped
½ cup cheddar cheese, shredded

Press the Steam/Cook button on the rice cooker and add the sausage. Stir to crumble, close the lid and sauté for 10 minutes, opening the lid occasionally and breaking up any big pieces. Toss in the potatoes and butter, give it a quick stir, close the lid and Steam/Cook for 7 or 8 minutes. Add the eggs, green onions and cheese, and stir to combine.

Close the lid and Steam/Cook for 10 minutes, opening the lid once or twice to gently scramble the scramble. Use the serving spatula to scoop the scramble onto individual plates.

*WHERE IS IT? You can find pre-cooked frozen hash browns in bags next to frozen French fries and other potatoes in the freezer section of your grocery store.

irish potatoes & eggs

HAVE ON HAND: 1 TBSP BUTTER, SALT & PEPPER | SERVES 4

Make this your lucky day by discovering how fast and easy this recipe cooks into a satisfying breakfast. You will feel like the Leprechaun who found his nonstick pot of gold.

2 cups pre-cooked frozen Potatoes O'Brien*, thawed
6 large eggs, beaten with a dash of salt and pepper
¼ cup half and half cream
½ cup Dubliner or white cheddar cheese, shredded
1 teaspoon fresh parsley, minced

Place the butter in the inner pot of the rice cooker and press the Steam/Cook button. Melt the butter and add the potatoes. Stir and sauté until browned. Whisk the cream into the eggs and pour the eggs over the potatoes. Toss in the remaining ingredients, close the lid and Steam/Cook for 12 to 14 minutes, or until the eggs are set. Use the serving spatula to scoop the eggs onto individual plates.

*WHERE IS IT? Potatoes O'Brien are a mixture of chopped potatoes, onions and green peppers. You can find them in the freezer section of your grocery store.

greek scramble

HAVE ON HAND: 1 TBSP BUTTER, SALT & PEPPER | SERVES 4

When Socrates knew he had a heavy schedule of philosophic discussions on his schedule, he always made a point of eating a fortifying breakfast. Give yourself a leg up with this quick and healthy start to your day.

¼ cup fresh red bell pepper, finely diced
1 cup baby spinach leaves, cleaned
8 kalamata olives, pitted and chopped
6 eggs, beaten with a dash of salt and pepper
½ cup feta cheese, crumbled

Place the butter in the inner pot of the rice cooker and press the Steam/Cook button. Melt the butter, stirring occasionally. Add the bell pepper and sauté for about 4 minutes, stirring often. Toss in the spinach and olives and continue sautéing until the spinach and bell pepper are softened. Pour the eggs over the vegetables and scatter the cheese over the eggs.

Close the lid and Steam/Cook, opening the lid once or twice to gently scramble the scramble. Cook 12 to 14 minutes, or until the eggs are done. Use a serving spatula to scoop the scramble onto individual plates.

tex-mex breakfast burrito

HAVE ON HAND: SALT & PEPPER | SERVES 4

This is one of those burritos that can be altered to suit your fancy...or your casual. Throw in some cilantro, add chopped yellow onions or tuck avocados inside. We don't really think you can go wrong with this one!

4 soft-taco size flour tortillas
¼ lb. chorizo sausage, uncooked
6 eggs, beaten with a dash of salt and pepper
1 cup Mexican cheese blend, shredded
1 cup medium-hot salsa

Wrap the tortillas in aluminum foil, place in the Steam Tray of the rice cooker and set aside. Press the Steam/Cook button and add the sausage to the inner pot. Stir to crumble, close the lid and sauté for a few minutes, opening the lid occasionally and breaking up any big pieces. Toss in the eggs and cheese and give it a quick stir.

Close the lid and Steam/Cook for 6 to 8 minutes, opening the lid and occasionally scrambling the eggs. Place the Steam Tray with the tortillas into the cooker and close the lid. Continue cooking for 6 to 8 minutes, or until the eggs are set. Scoop the eggs into the heated tortillas, top with a spoonful of salsa and roll-up the tortillas, burrito style.

real men love lorraine

HAVE ON HAND: 2 TBSP BUTTER, SALT & PEPPER | SERVES 4

Since the typical pastry shell is omitted in this quiche, try splitting croissants and placing a wedge of this yummy quiche inside. Sort of a real-man-breakfast-bonanza.

6 large eggs
¼ teaspoon ground nutmeg
¼ lb. fully cooked smoked ham, cut in thin
    matchstick pieces
1 large shallot, peeled and chopped
1 cup Swiss cheese, shredded

Beat the eggs with the nutmeg and a dash of salt and pepper. Place the butter in the inner pot of the rice cooker and press the Steam/Cook button. Melt the butter and add the ham and shallots. Stir and sauté for about 4 minutes, stirring occasionally. Toss in the eggs and scatter the cheese over the top.

Close the lid and Steam/Cook for 12 to 14 minutes, or until the eggs are set. Slide the quiche onto a large serving plate, cut into wedges and serve at once.

hawaiian hash with maui onions & spam®

HAVE ON HAND: 3 TBSP BUTTER, SALT & PEPPER | SERVES 4

Sheezam...yes, it's Spam®, all dressed up and ready for a luau, or maybe your breakfast! You can substitute cooked, cubed chicken breast or cooked shrimp in this island hash.

½ small Maui or yellow onion, peeled and diced
2 russet potatoes, peeled and diced small
½ cup pre-chopped red and green bell pepper*
1 can Spam®, diced
½ cup pineapple, diced

Place the butter in the inner pot of the rice cooker and press the Steam/Cook button. Melt the butter and add the potatoes. Stir and sauté for about 4 minutes. Toss in the onions and peppers and continue cooking, stirring frequently, for about 1 minute. Add the Spam, pineapple and salt and pepper to taste and cook until the hash is very well-browned and the potatoes are done.

*WHERE IS IT? The produce aisle is packed with time-saving shortcut goodies. Check out bags of pre-chopped peppers, sliced or chopped fruit, mixed veggies like peppers, celery and onion, as well as pre-washed and bagged salad greens. Notice that we said "time-saving short cuts," however, not "money-saving short cuts," because you will pay a little more for such produce luxuries. But, you're worth it!

authentic goldilocks porridge with berries

HAVE ON HAND: 2 CUPS WATER, A PINCH OF BROWN SUGAR | MAKES 4 BEARY GOOD SERVINGS

We're on to that house-crasher girl – she was trying to get to this delicious morning porridge, of course.

1 cup white or brown rice farina (or try yellow
    polenta)
1 cup lowfat milk
½ cup fresh strawberries, sliced
¼ cup sour cream
2 tablespoons clover honey

Place the farina in the inner pot of the rice cooker and stir in the milk and water. Close the lid and Steam/Cook for 10 minutes, opening the lid and stirring occasionally. Spoon the porridge into 4 bowls and top each with strawberries, sour cream and honey. If you're one of those types who needs more, more, more...add a pinch of brown sugar, as well. Makes 4 beary good servings.

almond, almond, almond steel cut oatmeal

HAVE ON HAND: 3 CUPS WATER, A PINCH OF SALT, 4 TBSP BUTTER | SERVES 4

If you have a thing for almonds, and there are many of us who do, this is your go-to recipe.

1 cup sweetened vanilla almond milk
1 teaspoon pure almond extract
3 tablespoons clover honey
1 cup steel cut oats
¼ cup toasted almonds, chopped

Place the almond milk, almond extract, honey, water and a pinch of salt into the inner pot of the rice cooker. Close the lid and Steam/Cook until the mixture comes to a boil. Toss in the oats and give it a quick stir. With the lid open, Steam/Cook for 30 minutes, stirring occasionally. Switch the cooker to Keep Warm mode, close the lid and let the oats stand for 10 to 20 minutes to finish cooking. Serve hot in bowls with a tablespoon of butter and a scattering of toasted almonds.

cinnamon & raisin morning rice

HAVE ON HAND: 4 TBSP BUTTER | SERVES 4

Leftover rice is a problem that we should discuss. Frankly, you feel too guilty to throw it away, but on the other hand, you're not quite sure what to do with it. Consider your "rice dilemma" solved here: Toss leftover rice with milk, sugar, raisins and cinnamon; pop it into the cooker and soak overnight. Heat it in the morning, and you're home free. Now, if you could only train the dog to start the coffee…

2 cups cooked white rice
2½ cups lowfat milk
¼ cup brown sugar, plus more if needed
¼ cup golden raisins
½ teaspoon cinnamon

Combine all ingredients, except the butter, in the inner pot of the rice cooker and stir lightly. Cover with plastic wrap and let stand in the refrigerator overnight. In the morning, give it a quick stir. Check the bottom of the inner pot to ensure it is clear of any debris before placing it in the cooker.

Close the lid and Steam/Cook until the rice is thick and creamy, about 10 to 15 minutes. Serve in bowls with a tablespoon of butter and additional brown sugar, if desired.

apple pie oats & raisins

HAVE ON HAND: 6 TBSP BUTTER, 3 CUPS WATER, A PINCH OF SALT, A FEW PINCHES OF BROWN SUGAR | SERVES 4

If you don't feel like dealing with peeling and dicing an apple because you're late for work already, core the apple, cut in large pieces and let your food processor or mini-chopper finish the job.

1 small apple, peeled and diced
½ cup raisins
½ teaspoon ground apple pie spice
1½ cups regular rolled oats
3 tablespoons maple syrup

Place 2 tablespoons of butter in the inner pot of the rice cooker and press the Steam/Cook button. Melt the butter and add the apples, raisins and spice, stirring often as the mixture sautés. Toss in the water and a pinch of salt, close the lid and Steam/Cook until the mixture boils. Add the oats and maple syrup and give it a quick stir.

With the lid open, Steam/Cook for 5 minutes, stirring occasionally. Turn off the cooker, close the lid and let stand for 2 to 3 minutes to finish cooking. Serve in bowls with a tablespoon of butter and a sprinkling of brown sugar on top.

southwestern breakfast tamale in a bowl

HAVE ON HAND: ¼ CUP BUTTER, 2½ CUPS WATER, PINCH SALT | SERVES 4

Tamale-making is a time-consuming, energy-draining venture. If you have a few days and a bunch of patience, you can impress your guests with fabulous tamales. Or, you can skip the drudgery, make this short-cut tamale dish, and knock the socks off your family and friends. It's up to you.

1 cup heavy cream
4.5 oz. can chopped green chilies
3 tablespoons clover honey
1 cup canned sweet corn, drained
1 cup yellow cornmeal

Place the butter in the inner pot of the rice cooker and press the Steam/Cook button. Melt the butter and add the cream, chilies, honey, corn and cornmeal, stirring well. Add the water and give it a good stir to ensure there are no lumps and the mixture is well-combined. Close the lid and cook for 12 minutes, opening the lid and stirring occasionally to prevent clumping and sticking.

Switch the cooker to the Keep Warm mode and let stand for 5 minutes, or up to 1 hour, or until the consistency is to your liking. Your breakfast tamale will get creamier the longer it sits. Serve in bowls with butter and honey or as a side dish with eggs.

sourdough pepper jack strata

HAVE ON HAND: 2 TBSP BUTTER, DIVIDED, SALT & PEPPER | SERVES 4

Cheesy, eggy and delish! And, don't worry about the iron-packed Swiss chard...it's slightly bitter flavor is absorbed by the other good stuff in this recipe.

1 medium yellow onion, peeled and chopped
1 cup Swiss chard*, cleaned, stemmed and chopped
2 cups stale sourdough bread, cut in small cubes
1 cup pepper Jack cheese, shredded
6 eggs, beaten with a dash of salt and pepper

Place 1 tablespoon of butter in the inner pot of the rice cooker and press the Steam/Cook button. Melt the butter and add the onion and chard. Stir and sauté until the greens are softened. Stir in the bread cubes with the remaining 1 tablespoon of butter, add the salt and pepper to taste and sauté for 4 to 5 minutes. Scatter the cheese over the bread mixture and pour the eggs evenly over the strata.

Close the lid and Steam/Cook for 12 to 14 minutes or until the eggs are set. Use a serving spatula to slide the strata onto a large serving plate. Cut into wedges and serve at once.

*WHERE IS IT? Swiss chard is a dark green, leafy vegetable that you can find in the fresh produce aisle. If you can't find it or are intimidated by it, substitute fresh spinach instead.

oasis sunrise couscous

HAVE ON HAND: ½ CUP WATER, 6 TABLESPOONS BUTTER, DIVIDED | SERVES 4

Midnight at the oasis can't compare to this luscious sunrise surprise. Exotic dried figs, sweet fruit nectar and fragrant almonds cook into a tempting breakfast that any good sultan knows will keep his entire camp happy all day.

1½ cups mango nectar
¼ cup dried figs, chopped
½ teaspoon ground cardamom*
10-oz. box plain couscous
¼ cup toasted almonds, chopped

Place the mango nectar, dried figs, cardamom and water into the inner pot of the rice cooker and give it a quick stir. Steam/Cook until the mixture comes to a boil. Toss in 2 tablespoons of butter and the couscous, stir well, close the lid and turn off the cooker. Let the couscous stand for 5 minutes, open the lid and fluff with a fork. Serve in bowls, each topped with a tablespoon of butter and a scattering of almonds.

*WHERE IS IT? Ground cardamom, chock-full of rich, aromatic flavor, can be found in the spice aisle. It's right at home in Mediterranean dishes.

bacon & cream cheese portobellos

HAVE ON HAND: 2 CUPS WATER, SALT & PEPPER | SERVES 4

*Don't bother messing around with little spoons, trying
to pack little bits of stuffing into eensy mushrooms. Go
for the gold and stuff a couple of bad boy Portobello
mushrooms. Serve each mushroom wedge with buttery
crackers to catch any stuffing that tries to escape.*

2 large Portobello mushrooms, brushed clean
4 oz. package cream cheese, softened
¼ cup Parmesan cheese, grated
2 slices smoked bacon, cooked and crumbled
1 green onion, thinly sliced

Pour the water into the inner pot of the rice cooker.
Place the mushrooms, gill-side up, in the Steam
Tray, close the lid and Steam/Cook for 8 minutes. In
a small bowl, blend the remaining ingredients and
add salt and pepper to taste. After steaming, open
the lid, mound half of the cream cheese mixture
on top of each Portobello and smooth the top
and edges with a knife. Close the lid and continue
cooking for 3 to 4 minutes. Let cool slightly, place
the mushrooms on a serving tray and cut each
mushroom into 6 wedges. Pop the wedges into your
mouth or, if you're into elegance and charm, serve
the wedges with buttery crackers.

shrimp & green onion raviolis

HAVE ON HAND: SALT & PEPPER, 2 CUPS WATER, SOY SAUCE | SERVES 6

Sure, you could buy frozen potstickers to save a minute or two, but would you really want to miss out on these light and delicious little Asian ravs? Check these out before you veer off into that frozen food section.

1 lb. raw shrimp, deveined, shelled and minced
½ cup water chestnuts, minced
2 green onions, minced
2 teaspoons sesame oil*
24 small round potsticker wrappers

Mix together the shrimp, water chestnuts, onion, sesame oil and salt and pepper to taste in a small bowl. Place a small scoop of the mixture in the center of a potsticker wrapper. Dab the edges of the wrapper with water and cover with another wrapper, pressing the edges together to seal. Repeat with the remaining wrappers and filling.

Pour the water into the inner pot of rice cooker. Place the raviolis in the Steam Tray so they do not overlap, position the tray in the rice cooker, close the lid and Steam/Cook for 12 minutes. When done, remove the raviolis and serve with a little soy sauce on the side. Then, get ready to make another batch because everyone will be asking for more.

*WHERE IS IT? Sesame oil is a "must have" on my list – a little bit of this seasoned oil goes a long, long way. Look for it in the Asian food section of your store.

kansas city asian spareribs

HAVE ON HAND: 1 TBSP CANOLA OIL | SERVES 8 TO 10

What does Kansas city BBQ have to do with Asian garlic sauce? We're not going to tell – you'll have to prepare this amazingly delicious recipe to find out for yourself.

2 lbs. boneless beef spareribs, cut into small pieces
1 cup Kansas City-style barbeque sauce
½ cup orange blossom honey
1 tablespoon Asian hot garlic sauce
3 green onions, thinly sliced

Pour the oil in the inner pot of the rice cooker and press the Steam/Cook button. Heat the oil and add the spareribs. Stir and sauté until well-browned. Toss in the remaining ingredients, except the green onions, and give everything a quick stir.

Close the lid and Steam/Cook for 15 to 20 minutes, or until the spareribs are cooked through and the sauce is hot and bubbly. Serve on a platter and garnish with the green onions.

aloha cocktail franks

HAVE ON HAND: DECORATIVE PARTY TOOTHPICKS | MAKES ABOUT 32

What is it with the "little franks on toothpicks" attraction? Frankly, we think they're addictive...in a great way. We want more.

½ cup orange marmalade
1 cup smoky barbeque sauce
10 oz. can pineapple chunks, drained, juice reserved
2 1 lb. packages smoked cocktail franks
2 green bell peppers, seeded and cut into chunks

Toss the orange marmalade, barbeque sauce and pineapple juice into the inner pot of the rice cooker and give it a quick stir. Close the lid and Steam/Cook for about 8 minutes. Add the cocktail franks and continue cooking for 5 minutes, or until the franks are hot and the sauce is bubbly. Assemble little kebobs of franks, pineapple and green peppers on the party toothpicks and serve right away.

sausage savories with onions & peppers

HAVE ON HAND: 2 TBSP CANOLA OIL, SALT & PEPPER | SERVES 8 TO 10

Invited to a pot-luck party, but no time to cook the day of? No worries, just make this scrumptious crowd pleaser the day before and carry it to the party in its own heating vessel. Plug in your rice cooker and re-heat the sausages, put out a basket of sliced baguette, spoon the mustard sauce in a small bowl and les le bon temps roulelet.

2 lbs. assorted fully-cooked sausages,
    cut into 1-inch pieces
6 oz. package pre-sliced mixed bell peppers
1 medium white onion, peeled and thinly sliced
1 jar aioli garlic mustard sauce* (or other spicy
    dipping sauce)
2 French bread baguettes, cut into ½-inch slices

Pour the oil into the inner pot of the rice cooker and press the Steam/Cook button. Heat the oil and add the onions and bell peppers. Stir and sauté until softened and slightly caramelized, about 5 minutes. Toss in the sausage, add salt and pepper and give it a quick stir. Close the lid and Steam/Cook until the sausages are hot through, about 8 to 10 minutes. Serve with a basket of sliced French bread and a small bowl of the aioli garlic mustard sauce.

*WHERE IS IT? Aioli garlic mustard sauce is a sassy, mustard/mayo sauce and you can find it near the fancy mustards or other gourmet sauces. For a switch, try a hearty mustard spread or, in a pinch, even mango chutney.

mandarin mushroom pops

HAVE ON HAND: 1 TBSP CANOLA OIL, ¼ CUP WATER | SERVES 8 TO 10

Spear a few...or a lot... and pop them in your mouth!

4 cups tiny button mushrooms, cleaned
1 cup Mandarin sauce*
1 teaspoon garlic, minced (fresh or from a jar)
1 teaspoon fresh cilantro, chopped
½ teaspoon crushed red pepper

Pour the oil into the inner pot of the rice cooker. Press the Steam/Cook button and heat the oil. Add the mushrooms and sauté until they begin to soften. Toss in the remaining ingredients, add the water, close the lid and cook for 5 to 10 minutes, or until the sauce is hot and bubbly. Scoop into a bowl and serve with party toothpicks or fondue forks.

*WHERE IS IT? Several food manufacturers produce Mandarin sauce. You can find it in the Asian food section of your grocery store.

fiery roasted tomato & italian sausage dip

HAVE ON HAND: SALT & PEPPER | SERVES 8 TO 10

This fiery-spicy dip may set your eyebrows aflame, but it's totally worth it.

½ lb. bulk Italian-spiced pork sausage, uncooked
2 15 oz. cans diced fire-roasted tomatoes with
    green chilies, drained, ¼ cup juice retained
8 oz. package cream cheese, softened
2 cups jalapeño Jack cheese, shredded
A big bag chili-lime tortilla chips, for dipping

Place the sausage in the rice cooker, press the Steam/Cook button and sauté, stirring frequently, until browned, crumbly and completely cooked. Toss in the remaining ingredients, except the chips, and add salt and pepper to taste. Give it a good stir to combine.

Press the Steam/Cook button and continue cooking, with the lid open, for 5 to 10 minutes, stirring frequently, until the dip is hot and bubbly. Serve in a large, heatproof bowl with chips for dipping.

tomatillo chili cheese dip

HAVE ON HAND: SALT & PEPPER | SERVES 8 TO 10

This dip will be gone in a heartbeat after serving, so you might want to out-smart your guests and double the recipe from the get-go.

2 28 oz. cans chili without beans
1 cup tomatillo salsa (fresh or from a jar)
4 oz. package cream cheese, softened
1 cup Mexican cheese blend, shredded
10 oz. bag tortilla chips, for dipping

Toss all ingredients, except the chips, into the inner pot of the rice cooker, add the salt and pepper to taste, and give it a good stir to combine. Steam/Cook, with the lid open, for 5 to 10 minutes, stirring frequently, until the dip is hot and bubbly. Serve in a large bowl with chips for dipping.

mexican beer chipotle con queso

HAVE ON HAND: SALT & PEPPER | SERVES 8 TO 10

The beer adds a rich tang to this traditional queso. However, in order to fully taste-test the recipe prior to serving, you might want to get a 6-pack of beer and go at it from there.

1 cup chipotle chili salsa*
2 cups Mexican cheese blend, shredded
8 oz. package cream cheese, softened
¼ cup dark Mexican beer
10 oz. bag blue corn tortilla chips

Toss all ingredients, except the chips, into the inner pot of the rice cooker, add salt and pepper to taste and give it a good stir to combine. Steam/Cook, with the lid open, for 5 to 10 minutes, stirring frequently, until the queso is hot and bubbly. Serve in a large bowl with chips for dipping.

*WHERE IS IT? If you're lucky, you can find chipotle chili salsa next to the dips and sauces in your store's refrigerator case. If fresh salsa isn't on the horizon, you'll find it in jars in the Mexican food section.

bubbly bruschetta
with garlic french bread scoopers

HAVE ON HAND: 2 TBSP OLIVE OIL, BLACK PEPPER | SERVES 4 TO 8

Get ready to hand out sturdy napkins – these bruschetta are messy and we wouldn't like them any other way!

2 14.5 oz. cans diced tomatoes with basil, garlic
    and oregano, with juices
2 tablespoons capers
½ small red onion, peeled and diced
3 tablespoons balsamic vinegar
1 loaf garlic French bread, sliced and wrapped
    in foil

Toss all ingredients, except the French bread, into the inner pot of the rice cooker, add pepper to taste and give it a quick stir. Place the foil-wrapped bread into the Steam Tray and place the tray into the cooker.

Close the lid and Steam/Cook for 10 to 12 minutes or until the bruschetta mixture is hot and bubbly and the garlic bread is warmed through. Serve the bruschetta in a large bowl and spoon as a topping onto pieces of the warm garlic bread.

prosciutto-wrapped aegean spiced shrimp

HAVE ON HAND: 2 TSP LEMON PEPPER, 2 CUPS WATER | SERVES 6

A fancy name and an elegant, savory app… with very little actual work involved, which makes this our favorite kind of app.

12 large fresh shrimp, peeled and deveined
3 artichoke hearts, each cut into quarters
12 sprigs fresh dill
6 slices prosciutto*, halved lengthwise
1 lemon, juiced

Top each shrimp with a fourth of an artichoke heart, a sprig of dill, a squeeze of lemon and a dusting of lemon pepper. Wrap the prosciutto around each shrimp bundle, tucking in the ends to seal. Place the shrimp in the Steam Tray. Pour the water into the inner pot of the rice cooker, and place the Steam Tray in the cooker. Close the lid and Steam/Cook for 8 to 10 minutes or until the shrimp are pink and the artichoke hearts are tender.

 *WHERE IS IT? "Proscuitto" in Italian translates to a dry-cured ham that is very thinly sliced. Find it in the deli case or counter. A little bit goes a long way.

roman artichoke crostini

HAVE ON HAND: SALT & PEPPER | SERVES 6 TO 8

This creamy, rich spread is so incredibly inviting; studies have shown that it is difficult to walk away after just a few bites.

16 oz. can artichoke crowns*, drained and
    chopped
1 cup mayonnaise
1 cup Romano cheese, grated (or use Parmesan
    cheese)
7.5 oz. can diced green chilies
10 oz. bag toasted crostini

Toss all ingredients, except the crostini, into the inner pot of the rice cooker, add salt and pepper to taste and give it a quick stir. Close the lid and Steam/Cook, stirring frequently, until the cheese melts and the dip is hot and bubbly, about 10 minutes. Adjust the seasonings, if needed. Spoon into a serving bowl and serve with the crostini.

 *WHERE IS IT? Not to be confused with artichoke hearts, the crowns are the "meat" of the artichoke found on the bottom. Find crowns in the canned vegetable section or condiment section of your store.

asiago crab spread with sourdough baguette

HAVE ON HAND: SALT & PEPPER | SERVES 6 TO 8

This goes without saying, but we'll say it anyway: Don't skimp on the Asiago cheese. Buy it, taste it and you'll love it.

2 cups fresh crab meat, picked through for grit
1 cup Dijonnaise (mayo with mustard combo)
1 cup Asiago cheese, shredded
1 green onion, chopped
1 sourdough French bread baguette, cut into
    ½-inch slices

Toss all ingredients, except the French bread, into the inner pot of the rice cooker, add salt and pepper to taste and give it a quick stir. Close the lid and Steam/Cook until hot and bubbly, about 5 to 10 minutes. Spoon into a serving bowl and serve with the sliced baguette.

fabulous self-serve little red potato hors d'oeuvres

HAVE ON HAND: 2 CUPS WATER, SALT & PEPPER | SERVES 4 TO 6

Similar to the "little franks on toothpicks" fascination (see p. 23), some people become fixated on these yummy little potatoes. And, we say, the problem with that is what?

12 little red potatoes, washed
1 cup sour cream with chives
½ cup smoked ham, chopped
½ cup Swiss cheese, shredded
2 tablespoons fresh parsley, chopped

Cut the potatoes in half across the fat center, dust with salt and pepper and place in the Steam Tray. Pour the water into the inner pot of the rice cooker and place the Steam Tray in the cooker. Close the lid and Steam/Cook for 12 to 18 minutes, or until the potatoes are tender, but still firm. Scoop a small well out of the center of each of the 12 potato halves and arrange the potatoes on a platter. Mix the remaining ingredients in a small bowl and place around the potatoes, allowing guests to create their own fabulous hors d'oeuvre.

fancy a curry? coconut meatballs

HAVE ON HAND: 1 TBSP CANOLA OIL, ¼ CUP WATER, SALT & PEPPER | SERVES 8 TO 10

Talk about easy! This might be one of those secret recipes you don't divulge to anyone else ever – no matter what. Unless someone offers you a bribe of dark chocolate and then you should shift gears pretty fast.

1 lb. package frozen pre-cooked meatballs, thawed

11.5 oz. can coconut milk

2 cups unsweetened pineapple juice

1 tablespoon curry powder

2 tablespoons quick-cooking tapioca or tapioca flour

Pour the oil into the inner pot of the rice cooker and press the Steam/Cook button. Heat the oil, add the meatballs and sauté for about 2 minutes. Toss in the remaining ingredients, except the tapioca, add salt and pepper to taste and give it a quick stir. Mix the tapioca with ¼ cup water and immediately stir into the curry sauce. Close the lid and Steam/Cook for 15 to 20 minutes, or until the meatballs are hot and the sauce is thickened and bubbly. Stir again before serving. Serve with party toothpicks or fondue forks.

white on white chili

HAVE ON HAND: 1 TBSP EXTRA-VIRGIN OLIVE OIL, SALT & PEPPER, WATER, IF NEEDED | SERVES 4

Snowbound you may be, but this white chili will set you free....Let the snowplows dig out the other poor saps, I'm eating chili!

¾ lb. boneless, skinless chicken breasts, cut into
　　½-inch pieces
8 oz. jar tomatillo salsa
10.75 oz. can condensed cream of chicken soup
2 15 oz. cans baby white beans, drained
1 cup chicken broth

Pour the oil into the inner pot of the rice cooker and press the Steam/Cook button. Add the chicken and sauté a few minutes until lightly browned. Toss in the remaining ingredients and give it a quick stir. Close the lid and Steam/Cook for 10 minutes. Open the lid, add salt and pepper to taste, and cook for an additional 5 to 10 minutes, or until the chili is cooked to the consistency you like. Add a little water, if needed to thin.

smokin' hot chipotle vegetarian chili

HAVE ON HAND: 1 TBSP EXTRA-VIRGIN OLIVE OIL, SALT & PEPPER | SERVES 4

A smokin' hot chili that will make a grown man cry. Vary the heat by the number of chipotles you add to the pot.... Add a little less...add a few more...or the whole can, go on, I dare ya! This chili uses Tempeh, a vegan protein powerhouse made from soybeans and grains. It has the texture of ground beef and takes on the flavors of its neighboring ingredients....what a pal.

8 ounces crumbled Tempeh*
2 15 oz. cans diced fire-roasted tomatoes with
      garlic, with juices
2 to 3 canned whole chipotle chilies, chopped,
      with 2 to 3 tbsps adobo sauce from can
28 oz. can kidney beans, drained
1 cup vegetable broth

Pour the oil into the inner pot of the rice cooker and press the Steam/Cook button. Heat the oil briefly and add the tempeh; sauté about 3 minutes. Toss in the remaining ingredients, add salt and pepper to taste and give it a quick stir. Close the lid and Steam/Cook for 10 minutes. Open the lid, stir and cook for an additional 5 to 10 minutes, or until the chili is done, adding more broth or water to thin the chili, if necessary.

*WHERE IS IT? Tempeh will be in the refrigerator case in your natural health food aisle at the store. If you can't find it or it's been a long day and you don't feel like experimenting with the unknown, ground chicken or turkey work equally well.

tuxedo chili

HAVE ON HAND: SALT & PEPPER, WATER, IF NEEDED | SERVES 4

You're in your tux, you're at a fancy dress ball, you look great, but the little watercress sandwiches just aren't doing it for you. Time to make your excuses to the Countess and sneak home to whip up a batch of black and white bean chili. Ready in 20 minutes, it makes the perfect midnight snack...and you're already dressed!

¾ lb. ground Italian spiced pork sausage, uncooked
8 oz. jar mild salsa
1 cup chicken broth
15 oz. can black beans, drained
15 oz. can white beans, drained

Place the sausage in the inner pot of the rice cooker, press the Steam/Cook button and sauté the pork until browned. Stir occasionally as the sausage sautés. Toss in the remaining ingredients, add salt and pepper to taste and give it a quick stir. Close the lid and Steam/Cook for 10 minutes. Open the lid, stir and cook for an additional 5 to 10 minutes, or until the chili is done, adding broth or water, if necessary.

cumin turkey & roasted sweet corn chili

HAVE ON HAND: 1 TBSP CANOLA OIL, SALT & PEPPER, WATER, IF NEEDED | SERVES 4

Serve this light, yet substantial chili on a cool autumn day. The roasted corn just screams "Fall" and the salsa verde takes it to a whole different level. Serve it with corn bread for a "corn-u-copia" of flavor. (Sorry – couldn't resist the pun.)

¾ lb. ground turkey
28 oz. can crushed tomatoes, with juices
8 oz. jar salsa verde
16 oz. package frozen roasted sweet corn*
1½ teaspoons ground cumin

Pour the oil into the inner pot of the rice cooker and press the Steam/Cook button. Heat the oil briefly and add the ground turkey; sauté until lightly browned. Toss in the remaining ingredients, add salt and pepper to taste and give it a quick stir. Close the lid and Steam/Cook for 10 minutes. Open the lid, stir and cook for an additional 5 to 10 minutes, or until the chili is done, adding liquid if necessary.

 *WHERE IS IT? If you can't find frozen roasted sweet corn in your grocery store freezer case, grab anything with corn…regular frozen corn, canned corn or southwestern canned corn. Adapt, improvise and overcome.

the quickest classic chili on the planet

HAVE ON HAND: 1 TBSP CANOLA OIL, WATER, IF NEEDED | SERVES 4

The game starts in an hour, folks will begin arriving soon and you have just burned the chicken wings beyond recognition. No worries, this classic chili is ready in twenty, using ingredients you most likely have on hand. Just remember to mess up the kitchen a bit; you don't want to make it look too easy.

1 lb. lean ground beef
1.5 oz. package chili seasoning mix, divided
2 28 oz. cans chopped tomatoes, with juice
2 15 oz. cans pinto beans, drained
1½ cups beef broth

Pour the oil into the inner pot of the rice cooker and press the Steam/Cook button. Heat the oil briefly, add the ground beef and half of the chili seasoning packet and sauté until the beef is lightly browned. Toss in the remaining ingredients including the remaining seasoning mix and give it a quick stir.

Close the lid and Steam/Cook for 10 minutes. Open the lid and add salt and pepper to taste. Stir and cook for an additional 5 to 10 minutes, or until the chili is done, adding more broth or water, if needed.

cantonese shrimp wonton soup

HAVE ON HAND: SALT & PEPPER | SERVES 6

Take the family on a quick trip to China, and don't forget to pack the chopsticks to pluck these delightfully flavorful wontons from the deliciously light broth. Make sure you pick up a souvenir for Aunt Betty... you know how she gets.

1½ teaspoons garlic, minced (fresh or from a jar)
2 teaspoons minced fresh ginger
8 cups chicken broth
16-20 oz. package frozen Chinese stir-fry
    vegetables
12 oz. package frozen shrimp wontons, thawed

Place the garlic and ginger in the inner pot of the rice cooker and press the Steam/Cook button. Add the chicken broth, close the lid and let the soup come to a simmer. Toss in the vegetables, wontons and salt and pepper to taste. Close the lid and Steam/Cook for about 10 minutes, or until the wontons are cooked through and the soup is hot.

triple b-best beef & barley soup

HAVE ON HAND: 1 TBSP CANOLA OIL, SALT & PEPPER | SERVES 4

Brand the beef and call in the ranch hands! Premium beef and tender pearl barley simmered together in a hearty soup will give your cowboys and cowgirls just what they need to get back in the saddle. Check your spurs at the door please; they really do a number on the kitchen floor.

1 lb. top sirloin steak, cut into ½-inch pieces
1½ cups pre-chopped carrots, peppers and onions*
10.5 oz. can French onion soup, plus 1 can water
½ cup pearl barley, uncooked
6 cups beef broth

Pour the oil into the inner pot of the rice cooker and press the Steam/Cook button. Heat the oil and add the steak pieces. Sauté until the beef begins to brown. Add the carrot mixture and continue sautéing until the carrots begin to soften, about 2 minutes. Toss in the remaining ingredients and add salt and pepper to taste. Give the soup a quick stir. Close the lid and Steam/Cook for 30 to 40 minutes, or until the barley is tender.

*WHERE IS IT? Look for containers of prepared chopped mixed veggies in the produce section of your grocery store. Substitute an onion, celery and pepper mixture in this recipe if you feel like living on the edge.

simple chicken tortilla soup

HAVE ON HAND: 2 TBSP BUTTER, SALT & PEPPER | SERVES 6

So simple to make, you could do it with your eyes closed......that is, of course, after you find your way out of the pantry. If you happen to have a lime on hand, cut it in wedges and pass it around the table.

4 cups chicken broth
16 ounces fresh mild pico-de-gallo*
2 cups cooked chicken breast, shredded
2 medium zucchini, halved lengthways and
    cut into ½-inch slices
Small bag tortilla chips

Place the chicken broth, pico-de-gallo and butter into the inner pot of the rice cooker, close the lid and Steam/Cook for about 5 to 10 minutes. Open the lid, add the chicken and zucchini, season with salt and pepper, close the lid and Steam/Cook for an additional 6 to 10 minutes, or until the zucchini is tender. Place a handful of chips in each of 4 bowls and ladle the soup over the chips.

*WHERE IS IT? Pico-de-gallo is a fresh salsa, chock-full of onion, tomatoes and cilantro. Find it in the refrigerator case next to the dips, spreads and cheese. Ole!

lamb & onion chutney stew

HAVE ON HAND: 1 TBSP CANOLA OIL, 1 CUP WATER PLUS ¼ CUP WATER FOR TAPIOCA, SALT & PEPPER | SERVES 6

Tell your office mates you picked up the recipe for this little gem on your last trip to the Great Continent.... while hunting for rubies...on camels...accompanied by a famous treasure hunter....okay, you get the picture.

1 lb. lamb stew meat, cut into ½-inch pieces
1 cup pre-cut fresh carrots and celery
12 oz. jar sweet onion chutney*
2 cups beef broth
2 tablespoons quick-cooking tapioca or
      tapioca flour

Pour the oil into the inner pot of the rice cooker and press the Steam/Cook button. Heat the oil and add the lamb. Sauté until lightly browned. Toss in the carrots and celery, chutney, and the beef broth. Add 1 cup of water and season with salt and pepper. Stir well to combine. Mix the tapioca with ¼ cup of water and immediately stir into the stew.

Close the lid and Steam/Cook for 20 minutes. Open the lid, stir and continue cooking for an additional 5 minutes, or until done, adding liquid and/or salt and pepper if necessary.

*WHERE IS IT? Chutney, a fruit or vegetable spread packed with tangy vinegar and spices, is typically sighted nestled next to specialty mustards and relishes in your grocery store.

russian sweet & sour beef borscht

HAVE ON HAND: 1 TBSP CANOLA OIL, 6 CUPS WATER, BLACK PEPPER | SERVES 6

Boris and Natasha thought about defecting, but then remembered that the Kremlin cafeteria served this Eastern European staple on Wednesdays. Try our super easy version, but watch out for spying eyes.

1 lb. beef top sirloin, cut into ½-inch pieces
16 oz. jar red cabbage, with juices
15 oz. can diced red beets, with juices
2 1 oz. pkgs. dried onion soup mix
¾ cup sour cream with chives

Pour the oil into the inner pot of the rice cooker and press the Steam/Cook button. Heat the oil and add the beef. Sauté until lightly browned. Add the water and all remaining ingredients, except the sour cream. Stir a bit and add pepper to taste.

Close the lid and Steam/Cook for about 20 to 25 minutes. Ladle into bowls and add a big dollop of sour cream to each.

smokey sausage & the bandit corn chowder

HAVE ON HAND: SALT & PEPPER, WATER, IF NECESSARY | SERVES 6

After a high speed, bone jarring, cross county boogie with Smokey on your tail, settle into a comforting bowl of this satisfying chowder. And, while you're at it, invite Smokey to dinner....you never know when you might need a favor.

1 lb. smoked turkey sausage, cut into 1-inch pieces
19 oz. can cream of potato with roasted garlic soup
2 15 oz. cans creamed corn
4 cups chicken broth
7.5 oz. can chopped green chilies

Toss all ingredients into the inner pot of the rice cooker, season with salt and pepper and give it a quick stir. Close the lid and Steam/Cook for about 15 minutes. Open the lid, stir and cook for an additional 5 to 10 minutes, or until the chowder is warm throughout, adding more broth if the chowder becomes too thick.

new year's lucky black-eyed pea soup

HAVE ON HAND: 1 TBSP CANOLA OIL, 3 CUPS WATER, 1 COPPER PENNY, OPTIONAL. BLACK PEPPER | SERVES 4

Southerners start their New Year with a good luck pot of black-eyed peas, as some say the beans resemble coins. They swell as they cook and hopefully, as go the beans, so goes your fortune! A penny in the pot is even luckier for the one who finds it in their bowl...unless you end up cracking a tooth...which doesn't seem lucky at all.... unless you fall in love with a rich dentist.

1 lb. smoked ham, cut into bite-sized pieces
2 15 oz. cans diced tomatoes with onion
      and garlic
1 package pre-cut collard greens*
2 15 oz. cans black-eyed peas, drained
3 cups chicken broth

Place the ham in the inner pot of the rice cooker and press the Steam/Cook button. Add the oil and stir for a few minutes. Toss in all the remaining ingredients, including the penny, if using, and add pepper to taste. Give it a quick stir. Close the lid and Steam/Cook for about 20 minutes. Serves 1 very lucky and 3 not-so-lucky New Year's hopefuls.

*WHERE IS IT? Collard greens are easy to find – go to the produce section and turn right. If you can't find collard greens, substitute spinach or other leafy greens. Whatever works for you...

hearty french onion soup with lentils & gruyere toast

HAVE ON HAND: 1 TBSP CANOLA OIL, 8 CUPS WATER, SALT & PEPPER | SERVES 6

You're hiking on the French-Swiss border; a freak springtime snow storm blows in and covers everything in white. You lose direction, you're soaked to the bone, all hope is lost...and then you smell it....the unmistakable aroma of French onion soup. And bread...toasting...with gruyere cheese. You're saved!

16 oz. pre-cut carrots, celery and onions
2 1 oz. pkgs. dried French onion soup mix
1 cup dry lentils, picked through and rinsed
6 slices hearty French bread
2 cups Gruyere* cheese, shredded

Press the Steam/Cook button on the rice cooker and heat the oil. Add the vegetables and sauté until softened, about 2 minutes. Toss in the French onion soup mix, the lentils, and water, add salt and pepper and give it a quick stir. Close the lid and Steam/Cook for about 25 to 30 minutes or until the lentils are tender.

Toast the French bread slices, top with the cheese and melt under the broiler for 1 minute. Place a piece of toasted cheese bread in the bottom of each bowl and ladle the soup over the top.

*WHERE IS IT? Gruyere cheese comes from Switzerland, is made from cow's milk, and has a nutty flavor. Look for it at the deli counter. You can use any Swiss cheese as a substitute if hunting for the Gruyere is too much adventure for you at the end of the day.

nor'easter chesapeake bay clam chowder

HAVE ON HAND: 2 TBSP BUTTER, 1 CUP WATER, PLUS WATER FOR CLAM JUICE | SERVES 6

Does anyone need to know that this creamy, rich soup starts with condensed soup? We'll never tell!

3 6.5 oz. cans minced clams, with juice
3 medium potatoes, peeled and diced small
2 10.5 oz. cans condensed cream of onion soup
1 cup heavy cream
½ teaspoon ground seafood seasoning

Place the butter in the inner pot of the rice cooker and press the Steam/Cook button. Add the potatoes and stir to coat. Drain the clams, reserving the juice, and add enough water to make 2 cups. Toss in the clams, clam juice with water, onion soup, cream, seafood seasoning and additional 1 cup of water. Give the soup a good stir to combine.

Close the lid and Steam/Cook for about 15 to 20 minutes. Open the lid, stir, and continue cooking for an additional 5 minutes, or until the potatoes are tender.

big fun on the bayou shrimp jambalaya

HAVE ON HAND: 2 TBSP BUTTER, 1 CUP WATER | SERVES 6

Shrimp that comes peeled and deveined is available in the freezer and fresh seafood sections of your grocery store. We think it's a lot nicer to buy our shrimp this way, rather than forcing our children to peel and devein the shrimp for us. Your rice cooker nicely cooks this Jambalaya ("Jahm-buh-lye-uh") in half the time it usually takes on the stove top. That's a 50 percent savings!

1½ cups medium-grained white rice

2 cups chicken broth

2 15 oz. cans diced tomatoes with onion and
	green bell pepper, with juices

Creole seasoning (1 to 2 teaspoons, as you like)

1 lb. large shrimp, peeled and deveined

Place the butter in the inner pot of the rice cooker and press the Steam/Cook button. Add the rice and stir to completely coat the grains. Stir in the remaining ingredients, except the shrimp, and add the water. Close the lid and press the White Rice button.

When done, press the Steam/Cook button and add the shrimp, give the jambalaya a quick stir, close the lid and continue steaming for a few minutes until the shrimp is cooked pink throughout.

vichyssoise aka your potato leek soup

HAVE ON HAND: 2 CUPS WATER, SALT & PEPPER | SERVES 3 TO 4

What to call this soup? If you're serving it chilled to snooty relatives, this is Vichyssoise. No question there. If serving this hot to a bunch of friends on a cold winter's day, it's simply Your Potato Leek Soup.

2 large leeks, white part only, cleaned very well
    and thinly sliced
2 medium russet potatoes, peeled and diced*
2 cups chicken broth
1 cup heavy cream
1 tablespoon minced fresh chives for garnish

Place the leeks, potatoes, chicken broth and water into the inner pot of the rice cooker and give it a quick stir. Close the lid and Steam/Cook for about 15 to 20 minutes, or until the potatoes and leeks are tender. Open the lid, stir in the cream and add salt and pepper to taste. Close the lid and continue cooking until the soup is hot and bubbly. Add additional cream or salt and pepper, if desired. Serve the soup either hot or cold in bowls garnished with minced chives.

WHERE IS IT? If you're pushed for time, buy frozen shredded or diced potatoes instead. Toss in 2 large handfuls of frozen potatoes for each raw potato. Toss in extra potatoes if you're a carb-lover.

creamy chicken vegetable & noodle soup

HAVE ON HAND: 1 TBSP CANOLA OIL, 2 CUPS WATER, SALT & PEPPER | SERVES 4

Chicken broth has long been acknowledged as a great cure for colds and flu, but with all the flavors of home neatly wrapped up in one yummy bowl of soup, it also cures the blues, home-sickness, and occasionally, even a broken heart.

½ lb. boneless, skinless chicken thighs cut into
    ½-inch pieces

14 oz. package frozen pre-cut mixed vegetables,
    thawed

10.5 oz. can condensed cream of chicken with
    herbs soup

4 cups chicken broth

2 ounces dry vermicelli or angel hair noodles,
    broken

Pour the oil into the inner pot of the rice cooker and press the Steam/Cook button. Heat the oil and add the chicken. Sauté until lightly browned. Add the vegetables and a dusting of pepper and sauté for a few additional minutes. Toss in the remaining ingredients and the water and give it a quick stir. Close the lid and Steam/Cook for 10 minutes, or until the noodles are tender, adding more broth, if needed.

hurried curried can can pumpkin soup

HAVE ON HAND: SALT & PEPPER | SERVES 6

Shake up your usual rotation of weekly dinners and serve this super easy soup that lives up to its name. It comes together in about 15 minutes. ...If you can open a can, you can. No prep, no big clean up and big, big props!

2 15 oz. cans unsweetened pumpkin
5 cups chicken broth
2 teaspoons curry powder
¼ cup clover honey
1 cup heavy cream

Toss all the ingredients, except the cream, into the inner pot of the rice cooker and give it a good stir to completely combine. Close the lid and Steam/Cook for about 8 minutes. Open the lid, add the heavy cream and salt and pepper to taste, close the lid and continue cooking until the soup is hot and bubbly, about 4 minutes.

basil's sun-dried tomato soup

HAVE ON HAND: SALT & PEPPER | SERVES 6

Historians argue as to who was responsible for bringing the tomato from South America to Europe, some say it was Cortéz and others say it was Columbus. Either way, he knew what was good for him...and everybody else.

2 15 oz. cans crushed tomatoes with basil and
    oregano
4 oz. jar sun-dried tomatoes in oil, drained and
    chopped
4 cups chicken or vegetable broth
1 cup heavy cream

½ cup fresh basil leaves, thinly sliced (chiffonade),
    divided

Toss the crushed tomatoes, sun-dried tomatoes, broth, and salt and pepper into the inner pot of the rice cooker and give it a quick stir. Close the lid and Steam/Cook for about 10 minutes. Add the heavy cream and half the basil leaves, close the lid and continue cooking until the soup bubbles. Serve in bowls topped with a sprinkle of basil leaves.

me-o my-o andouille sausage gumbo

HAVE ON HAND: 1 TBSP CANOLA OIL, 5 CUPS WATER, SALT & PEPPER | SERVES 6

Gumbo sounds like a party...so go ahead and have one. Or better yet, talk someone else into having one. Just show up with your rice cooker full of gumbo and add a ladle. The best part is knowing your clean-up will consist of one pot and one spoon.

14 oz. package frozen okra, thawed

16 oz. package frozen pre-cut bell peppers and
    onions, thawed

1 lb. smoked andouille sausage, cut into 1-inch
    pieces

2 10.5 oz. cans condensed creamy chicken with
    rice soup

Creole seasoning to taste

Place the okra, onion and bell peppers in the inner pot of the rice cooker and press the Steam/Cook button. Add the oil and toss the vegetables lightly as they cook for 2 minutes. Add the remaining ingredients and stir well. Add the water, salt and pepper to taste, and stir again to combine. Close the lid and Steam/Cook for 20 minutes or until the vegetables are tender.

king ludwig of bavaria's favorite pork & potato stew

HAVE ON HAND: 1 TBSP CANOLA OIL, SALT & PEPPER, 2 CUPS WATER | SERVES 6

When things didn't exactly go Ludwig's way – if he misplaced his crown, or had to attend his son's harpsichord recital – he usually ordered his band of merry cooks to whip up a batch of his favorite stew. This, of course, took days, with all that foraging for mushrooms and apple hunting, but it will only take you about 20 minutes. Lucky you.

1 lb. boneless pork shoulder, cut into ½-inch pieces
10.5 oz. can condensed cream of mushroom soup
1 cup apple juice
1½ teaspoons caraway seed
16 oz. package frozen baked potato chunks with
bacon, chives and sour cream*, thawed

Pour the oil into the inner pot of the rice cooker and press the Steam/Cook button. Heat the oil and add the pork. Sauté, turning often, until lightly browned.

Toss in the condensed soup, apple juice and caraway seeds and stir. Add the water, salt and pepper to taste and give it a quick stir. Add the potatoes, gently stir, close the lid and Steam/Cook for 15 minutes. Switch the cooker to the Keep Warm mode and let stand for 5 minutes, until the pork is cooked through and the potatoes are hot.

*WHERE IS IT? Look for frozen, pre-cooked potato chunks with bacon, chives and sour cream in the refrigerator case with other frozen potatoes/vegetables.

italian pesto meatball stew

HAVE ON HAND: 1 TBSP CANOLA OIL, SALT & PEPPER, 4 CUPS WATER | SERVES 6

This stew is so full of life-sized Italian flavors you will feel like you just spent the day cruising around Rome in your bright red Ferrari. Feel free to dream a little and add a few tablespoons of shaved Parmesan cheese... always a nice touch.

1 lb. package pre-cooked Italian-style meatballs (add more if you like)

1 small jar Italian sweet peppers in balsamic vinegar

2 14.5 oz. cans diced tomatoes with basil, garlic and oregano

15 oz. can cannellini beans, drained

½ cup basil pesto

Pour the oil into the inner pot of the rice cooker and press the Steam/Cook button. Heat the oil and add the meatballs. Sauté, turning occasionally, until lightly browned. Toss in all the remaining ingredients and add the water, salt and pepper to taste. Stir briefly to combine. Close the lid and Steam/Cook for 20 minutes or until the stew is hot and bubbly.

lemon & garlic chicken noodle soup

HAVE ON HAND: 1 TBSP CANOLA OIL, SALT & PEPPER | SERVES 6

You know when you walk into the grocery store and the mouthwatering aroma of rotisserie chicken wafts across the aisles, calling your name? Now you have one more reason to harass the folks at the deli counter..."are they done yet...are they done yet...are they done yet?"

½ lemon & garlic rotisserie chicken, meat
    removed from bones
16 oz. package frozen pre-cut carrots, celery and
    onions, thawed
10 cups chicken broth
½ cup fresh parsley, chopped
2 cups wide dried egg noodles, uncooked

Place the oil in the inner pot of the rice cooker and press the Steam/Cook button. Add the vegetables and sauté until just softened, about 3 minutes. Toss in the chicken meat and the remaining ingredients. Season with salt and pepper to taste and give it a quick stir. Close the lid and Steam/Cook for 10 to 15 minutes, or until the noodles are tender.

old-country secret family recipe kale & sausage soup

HAVE ON HAND: 2 TBSP EXTRA-VIRGIN OLIVE OIL, 2 CUPS WATER, SALT & PEPPER | SERVES 6

Be forewarned that when you make this soup for your friends, you WILL be asked for the recipe; it's that good. Claim it as a family secret, then reluctantly cave to their pleading......and collect on the favors now owed to you.

½ medium onion, peeled and chopped
1 lb. pre-cooked chicken garlic herb sausage,
    cut into bite-sized pieces
4 cups kale*, chopped
2 medium potatoes, peeled and chopped
8 cups chicken broth

Pour the oil into the inner pot of the rice cooker and press the Steam/Cook button. Heat the oil and add the onions. Sauté until slightly browned. Stir in the remaining ingredients and add the water. Add the salt and pepper to taste and give the soup a quick stir. Close the lid and Steam/Cook for 20 minutes, or until the potatoes are tender.

*WHERE IS IT? Kale is yet another one of those "greens" you hear so much about from your mom. Kind of a cross between green cabbage and curly lettuce, you can find kale in the produce section of your store. If kale is unavailable, substitute green cabbage for a fast fix.

herbed string beans with slivered almonds

HAVE ON HAND: 1 TBSP CANOLA OIL, 4 TBSP BUTTER, DIVIDED, 2 CUPS WATER, SALT & PEPPER | SERVES 6

Get your green on with these bright and fresh string beans! Zippy shallots and crunchy toasted almonds create a dish even your Uncle Herb would love.

1 shallot, peeled and thinly sliced
1 lb. fresh green beans, trimmed and left whole
2 teaspoons herbs de' Provence
¼ cup toasted almonds, slivered

Pour the oil into the inner pot of the rice cooker and press the Steam/Cook button. Heat the oil and add the shallot. Sauté, stirring often, until softened. Remove the shallot and pour the water into the inner pot. Place the green beans in the Steam Tray, cover with the cooked shallots, sprinkle with herbs de' Provence and a pinch of salt and pepper. Place the Steam Tray in the cooker. Steam/Cook for 10 to 15 minutes, or until the beans are tender. Spoon the cooked beans into a serving bowl, toss in the remaining butter and give it a quick stir. Adjust the salt and pepper to taste and top with slivered almonds.

tuna & tiny tomato tabouleh (aka tnttt)

HAVE ON HAND: 2 CUPS WATER, SALT & PEPPER | SERVES 2 TO 3

If your day has been like a keg of TNT, explosive and shattering, try popping this delicious dish into your rice cooker. This good-for-you tabouleh will re-trigger all your worn-out fuses.

1 cup bulgur wheat, uncooked
½ lb. fresh ahi tuna steak
1 cup small grape tomatoes, halved
1 medium cucumber, peeled and diced
¼ cup Italian salad dressing

Place the bulgur, water and a pinch of salt and pepper into the inner pot of the rice cooker, close the lid and Steam/Cook for 17 minutes. Place the tuna steak into the Steam Tray, open the lid and carefully place the Steam Tray into the cooker. Close the lid and continue to Steam/Cook for 5 or 6 minutes. When done, remove the tuna steak and set aside. Spoon the cooled bulgur into a serving bowl, toss in the remaining ingredients, except the tuna, and give it a quick stir. Slice the tuna steak thinly and place on top of the salad.

ooh-la-la potato salad

HAVE ON HAND: 2 CUPS WATER, SALT & PEPPER, ¼ CUP EXTRA-VIRGIN OLIVE OIL | SERVES 6

I see London, I see France…I see somebody's really tasty French potato and green bean salad. Change it up to a full meal deal by adding shredded, cooked chicken or diced ham just before serving.

1 lb. new potatoes, unpeeled, cut into bite-sized pieces
1 lb. fresh green beans, trimmed and cut in half
½ medium red onion, peeled and chopped
½ cup kalamata olives, pitted
1 tablespoon Dijon mustard

Place the potatoes, water and a pinch of salt into the inner pot of the rice cooker, close the lid and Steam/Cook for 10 minutes. Add the green beans and continue cooking for an additional 10 minutes. Place the potatoes and beans in a serving bowl and add the onion and olives. Whisk together the mustard and oil, season with salt and pepper to taste and toss with the vegetables. Serve while warm.

california turkey, avocado & blue cheese salad

HAVE ON HAND: 2 CUPS WATER, SALT & PEPPER | SERVES 4

How can you tell if a turkey is from California?....By its sun tan, of course.

3 large eggs
12 ounces turkey cutlets
3 ripe avocados, peeled and sliced
8 cups assorted salad greens
¾ cup blue cheese salad dressing

Pour the water into the inner pot of the rice cooker. Place the eggs, unshelled, in the Steam Tray, add the turkey cutlets and season with salt and pepper to taste. Place the tray into the cooker, close the lid and Steam/Cook for 12 minutes, or until the turkey is cooked through and no pink remains. Remove the eggs, cool, peel and slice into wedges. Cut the turkey cutlets into thin matchstick pieces. Arrange the greens on 4 plates and top each with the turkey, eggs, sliced avocados and a generous amount of dressing.

eat your squash!

HAVE ON HAND: 2 TBSP BUTTER, 2 CUPS WATER, SALT & PEPPER | SERVES 2

We know all about you. You haven't eaten your government-recommended number of vegetable servings today, have you? Wipe that guilty look off your face and eat your squash.

1 small acorn squash, peeled and cut into
    bite-sized pieces
1 tablespoon fresh sage, chopped

Place the water in the inner pot of the rice cooker. Place the acorn squash into the Steam Tray, sprinkle with sage and place the tray into the cooker. Close the lid and Steam/Cook for 20 minutes, or until the squash is tender. Spoon the cooked squash into a serving bowl and add butter, salt and pepper to taste.

valentino mushrooms with garlic & basil

HAVE ON HAND: 2 TBSP EXTRA-VIRGIN OLIVE OIL, 3 TBSP BUTTER, SALT & PEPPER | SERVES 6

These 'shrooms will make you swoon. Spoon them over a juicy steak or baked potatoes, or both!

8 ounces Italian brown mushrooms, cleaned, stemmed and sliced
2 cloves garlic, peeled and chopped
¼ cup dry white wine
1 teaspoon fresh basil, chopped

Pour the oil into the inner pot of the rice cooker and press the Steam/Cook button. Add the mushrooms and garlic, tossing lightly to coat. Close the lid and Steam/Cook for 7 minutes. Open the lid, add the butter, wine and basil and sauté for an additional 5 to 8 minutes, until the mushrooms are tender and slightly caramelized and much of the wine has cooked out.

cajun cuban corn on the cob

HAVE ON HAND: 2 CUPS WATER, ½ CUP MELTED BUTTER | SERVES 6

Think Cuban crooner meets Cajun cowboy; Latin spice with Louisiana flair. But seriously, this corn is so good you will find yourself creating menus around it....let's see, corn with grilled chicken, corn with pork chops, corn with waffles.

3 ears fresh corn on the cob, husked and silk removed
2 tablespoons Cajun spice blend
¼ cup cojita cheese, or other crumbly white cheese
1 lime, cut into 6 wedges

Break the corn cobs into pieces and place in the Steam Tray. Pour the water into the inner pot of the rice cooker and position the Steam Tray in the cooker. Close the lid and Steam/Cook for 10 to 15 minutes, or until the corn is crisp-tender. Transfer the corn to a serving bowl and smother with melted butter. Top with a sprinkling of Cajun spice and a smattering of cojita cheese. Serve with lime wedges.

italian stuffed artichokes steamed in white wine

HAVE ON HAND: 1½ TBSP EXTRA-VIRGIN OLIVE OIL, SALT & PEPPER, 1½ CUPS WATER | SERVES 2 TO 4

Stuffed and choked isn't a crime, it's a lovely dish made with white wine. Mix jarred pesto with good mayonnaise for a quick and easy dipping sauce.

2 large artichokes, stems removed and tips of
    leaves snipped
1½ cups bread crumbs
¾ cup Parmesan cheese, grated
2½ tablespoons jarred crushed garlic, divided
1 cup dry white wine

Remove any discolored leaves on the artichokes. Slice 1½ inches off the top of the artichokes and scoop out the fuzzy center of each with a spoon or melon baller. Mix together the bread crumbs, cheese, 1½ tablespoons crushed garlic and olive oil. Spoon the stuffing into the hollowed center and stuff the remaining crumb mixture in-between the leaves.

Set the artichokes in the inner pot of the rice cooker and dust with salt and pepper. Add the water, wine and 1 tablespoon crushed garlic. The artichokes will be slightly submerged. Close the lid and Steam/Cook for 20 to 30 minutes, depending on the size of the artichokes. If using very large 'chokes, increase the water and wine amounts, as the liquid will cook away. The artichokes are done when the leaves pull off easily. Serve while hot.

home sweet home sweet potatoes

HAVE ON HAND: 2 CUPS WATER, 4 TBSP BUTTER, SALT & PEPPER | SERVES 4

These potatoes will make you feel like a Norman Rockwell masterpiece...cozy and secure on a cold winter's eve. Serve mashed or just toss everything together in a large serving bowl....either way, forget about leftovers.

2 large sweet potatoes, peeled and cut into
    1-inch pieces
1 green apple, peeled, cored and diced
1 teaspoon ground allspice
¼ cup half and half cream

Pour the water into the inner pot of the rice cooker. Place the sweet potatoes and apple into the Steam Tray and sprinkle with the allspice. Position the Steam Tray in the cooker, close the lid, and Steam/Cook for 12 to 16 minutes, or until the potatoes are tender. Spoon the cooked potatoes and apples into a serving bowl and add the half and half cream and the butter. Mash by hand or with a mixer to a smooth consistency and add more cream if needed. Add salt and pepper to taste.

brussels sprouts with prosciutto & caramelized shallots

HAVE ON HAND: 2 CUPS WATER, 1 TBSP EXTRA-VIRGIN OLIVE OIL, SALT & PEPPER | SERVES 4

Don't be so darned judgmental! This recipe will turn even the staunchest sprout nay-sayer into a true believer.

4 slices fresh lemon
¾ lb. fresh Brussels sprouts, trimmed and halved
2 ounces prosciutto*, thinly sliced
1 large shallot, peeled and thinly sliced
2 tablespoons toasted pine nuts

Pour the water into the inner pot of the rice cooker and add the lemon slices. Place the Brussels sprouts into the Steam Tray. Position the Steam Tray in the cooker, close the lid and Steam/Cook for 10 to 15 minutes, or until the Brussels sprouts are just tender. When done, thinly slice the Brussels sprouts and set aside. Carefully drain the inner pot, wipe dry and replace into the cooker. Pour the oil into the pot and press the Steam/Cook button. Add the shallots and prosciutto and sauté, stirring frequently, until the shallots are lightly browned. Add the sprouts and salt and pepper to taste and stir lightly. Steam/Cook for 4 to 5 minutes to mix the flavors and heat the sprouts. Transfer to a serving platter and top with the toasted pine nuts.

*WHERE IS IT? Freaked out by proscuitto? Don't run away...proscuitto is Italian ham, sliced very thinly, and it adds immense flavor to everything it touches. Give it a whirl and see if you don't agree. You'll find it in the deli counter or pre-packaged with the refrigerated sliced meats.

lemon rosemary buttered potatoes

HAVE ON HAND: 2 CUPS WATER, SALT & PEPPER | SERVES 4 TO 6

A simply elegant dish for the culinary challenged.

8 red potatoes, cleaned and quartered
1 tablespoon chopped fresh rosemary
¼ cup butter, melted
1 lemon, juiced

Pour the water into the inner pot of the rice cooker. Place the potatoes in the Steam Tray and sprinkle with rosemary. Position the Steam Tray in the cooker, close the lid and Steam/Cook for 12 to 16 minutes, or until the potatoes are tender. Spoon the cooked potatoes into a serving bowl, toss with melted butter and lemon. Add the salt and pepper to taste.

jumpin' jack black beans!

HAVE ON HAND: SALT & PEPPER | SERVES 6 TO 8

When you accidentally spill your Bloody Mary into a bowl of black beans, you go with the flow and create a new 5-star recipe out of your tableside flub. At least, that's what we did. Serve this as a stand- alone side dish or scoop the beans into burritos and tacos; combine them with rice and salsa, or chill them and toss into a salad. A wonderful ending to the tableside flub story!

2 15 oz. cans black beans, drained
1 cup Bloody Mary mix
½ cup sour cream with chives
½ cup Mexican cheese blend, shredded
1 large ripe avocado, peeled and chopped

Toss the beans and Bloody Mary mix into the inner pot of the rice cooker and give it a quick stir. Close the lid and Steam/Cook for 6 to 8 minutes, until the sauce and beans are hot and bubbly. Transfer the beans to individual bowls and top each with sour cream, shredded cheese and avocado.

spicy shanghai noodles

HAVE ON HAND: 2 CUPS WATER, SALT & PEPPER | SERVES 4

Your taste buds will be tied up, thrown in a box and shipped to the Orient...aka Shanghaied, but you won't care! Try this with rice noodles, soba noodles, ramen noodles....there are oodles of noodles to choose from.

4 ounces dried linguini noodles, uncooked
1 package broccoli slaw mix
½ red bell pepper, thinly sliced
¾ cup soy sesame salad dressing
2 tablespoons Asian garlic chile sauce

Pour the water into the inner pot of the rice cooker, close the lid, press the Steam/Cook button and bring the water to a boil. Add the noodles, close the lid and cook until just tender, about 6 to 8 minutes. Drain the noodles in a colander and return to the inner pot. Press the Steam/Cook button and toss in the remaining ingredients; stir lightly. Add salt and pepper to taste and stir again. Serve warm.

wild cranberries + wild rice = wild salad

HAVE ON HAND: 3 CUPS WATER, SALT & PEPPER | SERVES 4 TO 6

Wild rice or wild cranberries? Either way, take a walk on the wild side. Easily change up this delish salad by using dried mango and a favorite tangy vinaigrette. Keep the dream alive.

1 cup wild rice, uncooked
⅓ cup dried cranberries
⅓ cup green onions, chopped
¾ cup raspberry vinaigrette
⅓ cup toasted pecans, chopped

Place the wild rice and water into the rice cooker, close the lid and press the Brown Rice button. When the cooker switches to the Keep Warm mode, let the rice stand for a few minutes. Turn off the cooker, fluff the rice with a plastic spatula and let the rice cool. Toss in the remaining ingredients and give it all a quick stir. Add salt and pepper to taste. Serve chilled or at room temperature.

champagne bulgur salad with apricots & italian parsley

HAVE ON HAND: 3¼ CUPS WATER, SALT & PEPPER | SERVES 6 TO 8

Ah yes, a champagne taste on a beer budget. Don't wait for a celebration to try this effervescent dish. If you can't find champagne vinaigrette, mix equal parts of champagne vinegar, olive oil and honey. This is something you definitely won't regret the next day.

2 cups bulgur wheat, uncooked
½ cup dried apricots, diced
¼ cup Italian flat leaf parsley, chopped
½ cup walnuts, chopped
¾ cup champagne vinaigrette

Place the bulgur and water into the rice cooker, close the lid and press the Brown Rice button. When the cooker switches to the Keep Warm mode, let the bulgur stand for a few minutes. Turn off the cooker, fluff the bulgur with a plastic spatula and cool. Toss in the remaining ingredients and stir lightly. Add additional salt and pepper to taste, if needed. Serve chilled or at room temperature.

snappy yams with brown sugar & ginger

HAVE ON HAND: 2 CUPS WATER, SALT & PEPPER, 4 TBSP MELTED BUTTER | SERVES 4

Technically, this is a vegetable dish, however these yams are so sweet and yummy, there could be some dessert-confusion involved.

2 large garnet yams, peeled and cut into 1-inch
    pieces
2 teaspoons brown sugar
2 teaspoons crystallized ginger, or 1 teaspoon
    ground ginger

Pour the water into the inner pot of the rice cooker. Place the yams into the Steam Tray and sprinkle with salt and pepper. Position the Steam Tray in the cooker, close the lid and Steam/Cook for 18 to 25 minutes, or until the yams are tender. Spoon the cooked yams into a serving bowl, toss in the remaining ingredients, add salt and pepper to taste and give it a quick stir.

moroccan quinoa, pistachio & date salad

HAVE ON HAND: 2½ CUPS WATER, ¼ CUP EXTRA-VIRGIN OLIVE OIL, SALT & PEPPER | SERVES 6 TO 8

Ali Baba and his forty thieves would have ransacked the Shah's castle to get their hands on this treasure.

2 cups quinoa, rinsed
1 lemon, juiced
3 green onions, sliced
¼ cup pistachios, chopped
¼ cup dates, chopped

Place the quinoa and water into the inner pot of the rice cooker and lightly stir. Close the lid and press the White Rice button. When the cooker switches to the Keep Warm mode, let the quinoa stand for a few minutes. Turn off the cooker, fluff the quinoa with a plastic spatula and let cool. In a small bowl, whisk together the olive oil and lemon juice and season with salt and pepper. Add the onions, nuts and dates to the cooled quinoa, toss in the salad dressing and toss to combine. Serve chilled or at room temperature.

baby spinach salad with wild rice & bacon confetti

HAVE ON HAND: 3 CUPS WATER, SALT & PEPPER | SERVES 6

Make the signs, decorate the floats and get ready to start the parade to celebrate a truly heroic salad! The scoop of rice in the spinach salad adds a layer of texture and provides the yummy dressing with an additional place to cling....always a good thing.

1½ cups wild rice and brown rice mix, uncooked
6 oz. bag fresh baby spinach leaves
½ to ¾ cup poppy seed dressing
6 pieces crispy-cooked bacon, crumbled
½ medium red onion, peeled and thinly sliced

Place the rice and water into the inner pot of the rice cooker, close the lid and press the Brown Rice button. When the cooker switches to the Keep Warm mode, let the rice stand for a few minutes. Turn off the cooker, fluff the rice with a plastic spatula and let cool. In a large serving bowl, toss the spinach with the rice and dressing. Top with the bacon and sliced red onion. Deeeelish!

terrifically tasty teriyaki tofu salad

HAVE ON HAND: 2¼ CUPS WATER, SALT & PEPPER | SERVES 4

If you haven't tried teriyaki baked tofu, you might be surprised that it actually tastes quite good. Slice it thinly or cut into small cubes – this powerhouse protein is most friendly when combined with other Asian flavors.

¾ cup brown rice (not instant)
6 oz. package teriyaki baked tofu*, cubed
3 tablespoons fresh cilantro, chopped
½ cup red bell pepper, thinly sliced
½ cup ginger sesame salad dressing

Place the rice and water into the inner pot of the rice cooker, close the lid and press the Brown Rice button. When the cooker switches to the Keep Warm mode, let the rice stand for a few minutes. Turn off the cooker, fluff the rice with a plastic spatula and let cool. Transfer the cooled rice to a serving bowl, toss in the remaining ingredients and give it a quick stir. Season with salt and pepper before serving.

*WHERE IS IT? Teriyaki baked tofu will be in the refrigerator case in the natural health food aisle of your grocery store.

chilled israeli couscous with golden raisins & orange ginger vinaigrette

HAVE ON HAND: 1 TBSP EXTRA-VIRGIN OLIVE OIL, 1 CUP WATER, SALT & PEPPER | SERVES 6 TO 8

Hip and healthy, this large round couscous is becoming a hot item in America. Take it to your next block party and become a legend in your own time....or at least in your own mind. Change it up with chopped tomatoes, cubes of mozzarella and Tuscany Italian dressing or try it with green onions, shitake mushrooms and sesame ginger vinaigrette.

1½ cups Israeli couscous
1 cup chicken broth
½ cup flat leaf Italian parsley, chopped
½ cup golden raisins
¾ cup orange ginger vinaigrette

Pour the oil into the inner pot of the rice cooker and press the Steam/Cook button. Add the couscous and sauté for 1 to 2 minutes, stirring twice. Add the chicken broth and water, close the lid and Steam/Cook for 12 minutes. When done, let the couscous stand for a few minutes. Turn off the cooker, fluff with a plastic spatula and let cool. Toss in the remaining ingredients and lightly stir. Adjust the flavors with salt and pepper to taste. Serve chilled.

el rey chicken & green chile potatoes

HAVE ON HAND: 1 TBSP OLIVE OIL, SALT & PEPPER | SERVES 4

The perfect go-to chicken dinner with 4 pretty basic ingredients. If you want to add tomato salsa and avocado as garnishes, you could refer to this as your "Gourmet El Rey" and fool most everyone into thinking you really know how to cook.

¾ lb. boneless, skinless chicken breasts, cut into
    1-inch pieces
10.5 oz. can cream of potato with roasted
    garlic soup
7 oz. can chopped green chilies, with juices
16 oz. package frozen baked potatoes with chives
    and sour cream, thawed

Pour the oil into the inner pot of the rice cooker and press the Steam/Cook button. Heat the oil and add the chicken breasts, turning once while browning. Stir in the remaining ingredients and add salt and pepper to taste. Stir again to combine. Close the lid and Steam/Cook for 5 minutes. Open the lid, stir and cook for an additional 5 to 10 minutes, until the chicken is cooked through completely and the potatoes are hot.

french dip torpedoes

HAVE ON HAND: 1 TBSP BUTTER, SALT & PEPPER | SERVES 4

Have you ever taken a bite of a lovely French Dip sandwich only to discover that the meat is so thick and tough that the whole thing falls into your lap? Let's talk prevention here – ask for extra-thin slices of roast beef at the deli counter. Cut the sliced beef into small squares before piling onto your bread. You'll never experience another beef-in-the-lap surprise.

1 shallot*, peeled and thinly sliced
1½ lbs. deli thin-sliced roast beef
10.5 oz. can French onion soup, undiluted
1 cup beef broth
4 torpedo rolls, split and warmed (or other large,
      soft sandwich rolls)

Place the butter in the inner pot of the rice cooker and press the Steam/Cook button. Heat the butter and add the shallot; sauté until the shallots are softened. Toss in the remaining ingredients, except the rolls. Add salt and pepper to taste and give it a quick stir. Close the lid and Steam/Cook for 5 to 8 minutes, or until the au jus is hot. Divide the beef between the 4 rolls and serve the au jus in small ramekins or soup cups for dipping.

*WHERE IS IT? Before you can find shallots, let's talk about what they are. Think of onions tossed with garlic and there you go. Look for shallots in the produce section by the onions.

burgundy beef with mushrooms

HAVE ON HAND: 1 TBSP BUTTER, SALT & PEPPER | SERVES 4

Similar to the luscious and delicious Burgundy Beef your mom used to make, except that this requires almost no effort and only a few ingredients. In fact, now that we think about it, the only similarity is in that luscious flavor.

1½ lbs. top sirloin steak, sliced into 1-inch strips
2 cloves garlic, peeled and chopped
4.5 oz. jar mushrooms, drained
½ cup red burgundy wine
12 oz. jar homestyle beef gravy

Place the butter in the inner pot of the rice cooker and press the Steam/Cook button. Heat the butter and add the beef and garlic and sauté until the beef is browned. Add the remaining ingredients and a pinch of salt and pepper to taste. Stir well to combine. Close the lid and Steam/Cook for 10 minutes until the beef is cooked through and the sauce is bubbly. Serve over rice, pasta or baked potatoes.

sizzlin' asian plum pork

HAVE ON HAND: 1½ CUPS WATER, 1 TBSP CANOLA OIL, SALT & PEPPER | SERVES 4

Have no fear when it comes to Asian cooking sauces! Sure, they may cost a bit of money, but they keep for months in the fridge and spark just about any cut of meat or poultry into something special. So worth it!

1 cup white rice
1½ lbs. boneless pork roast, cut into 1-inch pieces
12 oz. jar Asian plum sauce*
¾ cup catsup
½ cup pineapple juice

Pour the water into the inner pot of the rice cooker and add the rice. Press the White Rice button. When done, remove the cooked rice, place in a bowl and cover with foil to keep warm.

Clean the inner pot and add the oil. Press the Steam/Cook button and add the pork. Stir well and sauté for a few minutes. Add the plum sauce, catsup and juice and stir well. Add a pinch of salt and pepper and stir again. Close the lid and Steam/Cook for 10 minutes, or until the pork is cooked through. Serve the pork and sauce over the rice.

*WHERE IS IT? Asian plum sauce can be found in the Asian food aisle of your grocery store. Couldn't be easier!

orange sesame chicken with water chestnuts

HAVE ON HAND: 1 TBSP CANOLA OIL, BLACK PEPPER, ¼ CUP WATER | SERVES 4

Now that you have this fail-safe, easy recipe, "flag" it for those dinner party occasions when you have no clue what to serve.

1½ lbs. boneless, skinless chicken breasts, cut
      into 1-inch pieces
¼ cup orange marmalade
7 oz. jar hoisin sauce*
1½ teaspoons sesame oil
8 oz. can sliced water chestnuts, drained

Pour the oil into the inner pot of the rice cooker and press the Steam/Cook button. Heat the oil and add the chicken. Sauté, turning frequently, until lightly browned. Add the remaining ingredients, along with the water and stir well. Season with the pepper and give it a quick stir again. Close the lid and Steam/Cook for 10 minutes or until the chicken is cooked through. Serve over hot Asian noodles or rice.

 *WHERE IS IT? You'll find small jars of hoisin sauce right in line with other Asian sauces and specialty foods in the grocery store. Think of hoisin sauce as an Asian barbeque sauce, tangy and sassy.

pulled pork bbq loafers

HAVE ON HAND: 2½ CUPS WATER | SERVES AT LEAST 4 LOAFERS, MAYBE EVEN 6

You'll never guess why these hefty sandwiches are called "loafers," but they were created to please guys who sit around all weekend, watching ESPN and doing a lot of nothing. Add some pickles, a big bag of potato chips, and a case of dark beer as garnishes.

10 or 12-oz. pork tenderloin
1 cup purchased barbecue sauce
¼ cup bottled chili sauce
1 white onion, peeled and thinly sliced
4 to 6 large soft sandwich buns, split and toasted

Completely line the Steam Tray of the rice cooker with 2 large pieces of aluminum foil to create a spill-proof liner and lightly coat it with cooking spray. Place the pork tenderloin in the tray, drench with the barbecue and chili sauces and scatter the onions over all. Pour the water into the inner pot of the cooker, place the steamer tray into the cooker, close the lid and Steam/Cook for 25 to 30 minutes, or until the pork is cooked through and tender.

On a cutting board, shred the pork with a fork. Place the pork in a large bowl and stir in the remaining sauce from the Steam Tray. Don't be stingy with the sauce – sloppy and juicy is good here. Mound equal portions onto sandwich buns and serve with plenty of napkins and the above-mentioned garnishes.

bacon & cheese steak sandwiches

HAVE ON HAND: BLACK PEPPER | SERVES 4

Serve up these warm and cheesy steak sandwiches with a fresh green salad for a feel-good-about-yourself complete meal.

4 slices bacon, cut into small pieces
1 lb. sirloin beef steak*, sliced into thin strips
1 white onion, peeled and thinly sliced
4 oz. package cream cheese, cut into small pieces
4 hoagie sandwich rolls, split and toasted

Place the bacon in the inner pot of the rice cooker and press the Steam/Cook button. Stir and sauté for a few minutes until the bacon is almost cooked through. Add the beef and onions and sauté until the beef is browned, but pink in the center, about 1 minute.

Toss in the cream cheese and add black pepper to add some zip. Stir well to incorporate the cheese. Close the lid and Steam/Cook for 2 minutes. Spoon the beef and sauce mixture into the rolls and serve while warm.

 *WHERE IS IT? Sirloin steak is a tender cut of beef that slices easily if you freeze it briefly for about 20 minutes first. If you can't find a sirloin, look for a tenderloin or club steak at your meat counter.

street fish tacos with sesame sauce

HAVE ON HAND: SALT & PEPPER | MAKES 4 SERVINGS; 3 STREET TACOS EACH

When is a taco a "street taco?" Good question. You see, there are tacos and then there are other tacos. Tacos are usually good-sized and include fried corn tortillas, fried flour tortillas, or even fried wonton wrappers if you live in California. Street tacos, on the other hand, are small and made with steamed corn tortillas. Taco carts on the street sell street tacos, however you can also buy them in a restaurant or make them at home, all of which makes perfect sense.

2 cups chicken broth
1 lb. mild, white fish fillets
¾ cup sesame salad dressing, divided
3 cups Asian cole slaw salad mix
12 small corn tortillas, warmed

Pour the chicken broth into the inner pot of the rice cooker, add the fish to the Steam Tray and season with salt and pepper to taste. Close the lid and Steam/Cook for 15 minutes, or until the fish flakes easily. Remove the fish, cut into bite-sized pieces and gently toss with ¼ cup of the salad dressing. To assemble the tacos, fill each corn tortilla with fish and cole slaw and drizzle with the extra sauce.

coq au vin in one pan

HAVE ON HAND: SALT & PEPPER | SERVES 4

Label yourself a "true French gourmet chef" as you serve this with French bread for mopping up the extra sauce.

3 slices uncooked bacon, cut into small pieces
¾ lb. boneless, skinless chicken thighs, cut into
     1-inch pieces
2 shallots, peeled and sliced
4 ounces button mushrooms, cleaned
2 cups red wine

Place the bacon pieces in the inner pot of the rice cooker and press the Steam/Cook button. Stir and cook for a few minutes until the bacon is almost cooked. Add the chicken and sauté until it is lightly browned. Remove the chicken and bacon and set aside.

Add the shallots and mushrooms to the pot and sauté until they begin to caramelize, stirring frequently. Add the wine and salt and pepper to taste, stirring to deglaze the pot and scraping up any browned bits from the bottom of the pot. Toss in the browned chicken and bacon and give all of this another quick stir. Close the lid and Steam/Cook for 10 minutes or until chicken is cooked through completely. Spoon the sauce over the chicken to serve.

steamed mussels in white wine & basil

HAVE ON HAND: 1 TBSP EXTRA-VIRGIN OLIVE OIL, ¼ CUP WATER, 4 TBSP BUTTER, SALT & PEPPER | SERVES 4

Surprisingly, even our kids liked this dish. We heard something about "alien mussel life forms taking over the world" and then there was all the dipping of the bread into the sauce, which adds oh so much excitement. Score!

2 shallots, peeled and chopped
2 cups dry white wine
2 lbs. mussels, scrubbed and beards removed
2 tablespoons fresh basil leaves, chopped
1 French bread baguette, cut into thick slices and
     warmed in foil

Pour the oil into the inner pot of the rice cooker and press the Steam/Cook button. Heat the oil and add the shallots. Stir and sauté until softened. Add the wine and water, close the lid and bring to a boil in about 6 minutes. Toss in the mussels and basil, close the lid and Steam/Cook until all of the mussels have opened, about 6 to 8 minutes. Discard any mussels that have not opened. Remove the mussels to a serving bowl and stir the butter and salt and pepper into the wine sauce. Spoon the wine sauce over the mussels and serve with warmed French bread for sopping.

pork medallions in horseradish mustard sauce

HAVE ON HAND: 2 TBSP BUTTER, SALT & PEPPER | SERVES 4

Why would anyone label cuts of meat as "medallions" unless there is some kind of trophy involved? We're not sure exactly, but speaking of trophies, you'll bring one home with this recipe.

¾ lb. pork tenderloin, cut into ½-inch rounds
1 large shallot, peeled and sliced
1 cup chicken broth
½ cup heavy cream
3 tablespoons horseradish mustard*

Lightly dust the pork medallions with salt and pepper. Place the butter in the rice cooker and press the Steam/Cook button. Add the pork and sauté until each side is browned and the pork is cooked through, about 3 minutes per side. Transfer the pork to a plate.

Toss the shallot into the pot and sauté for a few minutes, add the chicken broth and cream and give it a quick stir. Allow the sauce to come to a boil, stirring often. Stir in the mustard, return the pork to the pot and switch the cooker to the Keep Warm mode, warming the sauce just until the pork is re-heated through, about 1 minute. Add salt and pepper to taste and serve right away.

*WHERE IS IT? You'll find zesty horseradish mustard right next to the condiments in your store. The "bite" of this sauce is strong, but that's what makes it so perfect with the mild pork. Go for it!

mandarin teriyaki salmon with fresh cilantro

HAVE ON HAND: 2 TBSP BUTTER, SALT & PEPPER, 2 CUPS WATER | SERVES 4

Easy to prep, delicious salmon...with no dirty pots or pans. Ya gotta love this recipe!

½ cup purchased teriyaki sauce
6 oz. can mandarin oranges, sliced, syrup
    reserved
1 small red onion, peeled and thinly sliced
4 6-oz. salmon fillets
1 tablespoon fresh cilantro, chopped

In a small bowl, combine the teriyaki sauce and mandarin orange slices with the reserved syrup and stir well. Cut 2 large pieces of foil and fold down the middle. Divide the onions between foil pieces and top each with a salmon fillet. Pour half of the orange teriyaki sauce over each fillet, add a tablespoon of butter, dust with salt and pepper and scatter cilantro on top.

Fold the foil over, leaving it slightly puffy to allow for steam expansion, crimp the edges to secure and place the packets in the Steam Tray. Pour the water into the inner pot and position the Steam Tray in the cooker. Close the lid and Steam/Cook for 10 to 15 minutes, or until the fish is opaque and flakes easily.

apple pie oats
& raisins

p. 17

shrimp & green
onion raviolis
p. 22

mexican beer
chipotle con queso
p. 27

the quickest
classic chili
on the planet
p. 37

cantonese shrimp
wonton soup
p. 38

simple chicken &
tortilla soup

p. 40

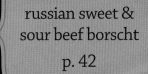

russian sweet &
sour beef borscht
p. 42

hurried curried
can can
pumpkin soup
p. 49

basil's sun-dried
tomato soup
p. 49

eat your squash!

p. 57

french dip
torpedos

p. 70

burgundy beef
with mushrooms

p. 92

pork medallions
in horseradish
mustard sauce

p. 79

pulled pork
bbq loafers

p. 74

busy night
spaghetti with
meatballs

p. 106

hungry hungarian
goulash

p. 107

bombay
chickpeas with
curry & vegetables

p. 108

penne pasta
with homemade
vodka sauce

p. 125

risi e pisi, pleasi!
(rice with peas,
please)

p. 130

wine-poached
pears with caramel

p. 131

thai ginger's world
famous coconut
rice pudding

p. 134

old-fashioned
bread pudding

p. 137

chocolate
chocolate chip
clouds

p. 138

medieval happy
hour mulled
apple cider

p. 141

knockyourtopoff chicken stroganoff

HAVE ON HAND: 1 TBSP EXTRA-VIRGIN OLIVE OIL, SALT & PEPPER, WATER, IF NECESSARY | SERVES 4

Named for the famous Russian figure skating coach who, with little time for cooking, created this quick and hearty dish to feed her hungry Olympic hopeful. Can you say Triple Salchow three times fast?

1 lb. boneless, skinless chicken breasts, cut into ½-inch pieces

2 10.5 oz. cans condensed cream of chicken and mushroom soup

2 cups chicken broth

6 ounces dried egg noodles, uncooked

8 oz. carton sour cream

Pour the oil into the inner pot of the rice cooker and press the Steam/Cook button. Heat the oil and add the chicken breasts. Stir and sauté until lightly browned, about 3 minutes. Toss in the remaining ingredients, except the sour cream, add salt and pepper to taste and give it all a quick stir.

Close the lid and Steam/Cook for about 15 minutes, or the chicken is cooked through and the noodles are tender. Stir frequently to prevent the noodles from sticking together. Add additional water if the sauce becomes too thick. Stir in the sour cream and cook for a few minutes to re-heat if necessary.

busy night spaghetti with meatballs

HAVE ON HAND: WATER, IF NECESSARY | SERVES 4

No chopping tomatoes, no peeling garlic and only one nonstick pan to clean...why wait for a busy night? Toss this together in about 3 minutes, pour yourself a glass of wine and your dinner prep is done. Ah, doesn't that feel good?

1 lb. package pre-cooked Italian-style meatballs

24-oz. jar purchased tomato basil spaghetti sauce*

1¾ cups red wine (or water)

8 ounces dry spaghetti noodles, uncooked,
    broken in half

½ cup Parmesan cheese, grated

Toss all ingredients, except the grated cheese, into the inner pot of the rice cooker, and give it a quick stir. Close the lid and Steam/Cook for about 15 to 20 minutes, or until the pasta is tender, stirring frequently to prevent the noodles from sticking together. Add additional water if the sauce becomes too thick. Spoon into individual bowls and garnish with the cheese.

*WHERE IS IT? Different types of spaghetti, marinara and pizza sauces are grouped together in one aisle in your grocery store and, typically, the noodles are within arm's reach. Very handy. If you already have a jar of spaghetti sauce with meat, mushrooms, peppers, or what-have-you, toss that in this recipe instead. It all works and that's what makes it so good.

hungry hungarian goulash

HAVE ON HAND: 1 TBSP EXTRA-VIRGIN OLIVE OIL, SALT & PEPPER | SERVES 4

Did you hear the one about the hungry Hungarian who couldn't find his goulashes..turns out his wife had traded them for stew meat to make his favorite dish, beef with paprika, for his birthday. The hungry Hungarian could not be mad at that, so instead he named his birthday treat after his boots. That's our story and we're sticking to it.

1 lb. beef stew meat, cut into small chunks
    (substitute 1 lb. chicken breast, cut into
    1-inch pieces)
2 tablespoons smoked Hungarian paprika*
2 15 oz. cans diced tomatoes with onions and
    green pepper, with juices
2½ cups beef broth
6 ounces dry egg noodles, uncooked

Pour the oil into the inner pot of the rice cooker and press the Steam/Cook button. Heat the oil and add the beef. Sprinkle the beef with the paprika and sauté until well-browned, turning occasionally. Toss in the remaining ingredients, add salt and pepper to taste and give everything a quick stir.

Close the lid and cook for 20 minutes, stirring frequently to prevent the noodles from sticking together. Open the lid and continue cooking for 10 to 15 minutes, until the sauce slightly thickens. Serve at once.

 *WHERE IS IT? You're asking why you should buy something like smoked Hungarian paprika, right? Give us the benefit of the doubt...you'll reach for this incredibly aromatic paprika again and again.

bombay chickpeas with curry & vegetables

HAVE ON HAND: 1 TBSP CANOLA OIL, SALT & PEPPER | SERVES 4

This dish sounds exotic, but the ingredients are simple to find in your store. Whisk through a few aisles to grab everything and you're out the door in about 5 minutes. If you're really energetic, toss a pre-made salad into your cart to round out this dinner.

16 oz. bag frozen broccoli, cauliflower and
    carrots, thawed
2 15 oz. cans chickpeas, drained (also called
    garbanzo beans)
1 tablespoon curry powder
½ cup mild salsa (preferably fresh)
1 cup vegetable broth

Pour the oil into the inner pot of the rice cooker and press the Steam/Cook button. Heat the oil and add the mixed vegetables. Stir and sauté until they just begin to soften, about 4 minutes. Toss in all remaining ingredients, add salt and pepper to taste and stir lightly. Steam/Cook for 10 minutes or until the curry is hot and bubbly.

braised beef short ribs & macaroni

HAVE ON HAND: 1 TBSP EXTRA-VIRGIN OLIVE OIL, SALT & PEPPER | SERVES 4

Any dish with shell macaroni counts as "kid-friendly" because kids can actually get this pasta onto their fork, unlike most noodles. Expect some clean plates!

1 lb. boneless beef short ribs, cut into 1-inch
    pieces
½ medium white onion, peeled and chopped
2 15 oz. cans stewed tomatoes, with juices
2 cups beef broth
4 ounces small shell macaroni, uncooked

Pour the oil into the inner pot of the rice cooker and press the Steam/Cook button. Heat the oil and add the onion and beef. Stir and sauté until lightly browned. Add the remaining ingredients and salt and pepper to taste. Stir lightly to break up any large tomato pieces.

Close the lid and Steam/Cook for 30 to 35 minutes, or until the beef is cooked and the noodles are tender.

lemony shrimp with cannellini beans

HAVE ON HAND: 3 TBSP BUTTER, DIVIDED, SALT & PEPPER | SERVES 4

Don't confuse "cannellini" with "cannelloni" or "cannoli." Confusion with these culinary names has been known to cause a conundrum for cooks.

2 cloves garlic, peeled and chopped
1 lb. shrimp, peeled and deveined
2 15 oz. cans cannellini beans, rinsed and drained
½ cup flat leaf parsley, chopped
1 lemon, juiced

Place the butter in the inner pot of the rice cooker and press the Steam/Cook button. Heat the butter, add the garlic and sauté for 30 seconds. Add the shrimp and sauté for 2 minutes. Toss in all remaining ingredients, including the remaining butter, and salt and pepper to taste. Gently stir to combine and Steam/Cook just until the shrimp is pink and the beans are hot and bubbly.

ginger orange pork chops with white rice

HAVE ON HAND: 1 TBSP CANOLA OIL, SALT & PEPPER, 1¼ CUPS WATER | SERVES 2

Fresh ginger has a major impact on food, so go to this recipe if you are a ginger-lover. If you're only halfway committed to the relationship, try 1 tablespoon of grated ginger instead.

2 tablespoons ginger, grated
2 1-inch thick boneless pork chops, dusted with salt and pepper
1½ cups medium grained white rice, uncooked
2 cups chicken broth
¼ cup orange marmalade, plus more for garnishing

Pour the oil into the inner pot of the rice cooker and press the Steam/Cook button. Heat the oil and add the ginger and pork. Sauté until the pork is lightly browned. Remove the pork from the cooker, place in the Steam Tray, cover and set aside. Place the rice, chicken broth, orange marmalade and water into the cooker and give it a quick stir.

Close the lid and press the White Rice button. When the cooker switches to the Keep Warm mode, gently fluff the rice, place the Steam Tray into the cooker, close the lid and let it all cook until the pork is cooked through. Serve the pork over the rice with a spoonful of marmalade on top.

the bok choy boys chicken

HAVE ON HAND: 1 TBSP CANOLA OIL, SALT & PEPPER | SERVES 4

Boys (and girls) will actually ask for this teriyaki noodle bowl simply because they'll want to say the name. If you're lucky, they might even eat it.

1 lb. boneless, skinless chicken breast, cut in
    ½ inch pieces
2 heads baby bok choy, chopped
14 oz. frozen Chinese stir-fry vegetables, thawed
1 cup teriyaki cooking sauce
8 ounces fettuccini noodles, cooked and drained

Pour the oil into the inner pot of the rice cooker and press the Steam/Cook button. Heat the oil and add the chicken. Sauté until lightly browned. Toss in the remaining ingredients, except the noodles, and add salt and pepper to taste. Stir well to combine.

Close the lid and Steam/Cook for 8 to 10 minutes, or until the chicken is cooked through and no pink remains. Add the noodles and toss again to combine. If you have any sesame seeds hanging around, scatter some over each serving as a garnish.

steak & sour cream stroganoff

HAVE ON HAND: 1 TBSP EXTRA-VIRGIN OLIVE OIL, SALT & PEPPER | SERVES 4

This is so amazingly easy and the results are so completely tasty, it makes you wonder if it might become illegal in the future. Assert your rights and enjoy.

1 lb. boneless top sirloin steak, cut into
    1-inch strips
2 10.5 oz. cans condensed cream of
    mushroom soup
2½ cups beef broth
6 ounces egg noodles, uncooked
1 carton sour cream with chives

Press the Steam/Cook button on the rice cooker and heat the oil. Add the beef and onion and sauté until browned. Add the soup and broth and stir well to combine. Add a pinch of salt and pepper to taste. Stir in the egg noodles, close the lid and Steam/Cook for about 15 minutes, or until the noodles are tender, stirring frequently to prevent the noodles from sticking together.

Add water or additional broth if the sauce becomes too thick. Just before serving, stir in the sour cream and cook for a few minutes to heat through.

stir-fry pork & black bean sauce with soba noodles

HAVE ON HAND: 1 TBSP CANOLA OIL, SALT & PEPPER | SERVES 4

Soba noodles are made of buckwheat, but don't let that bit of info scare you away. These noodles are good-for-you and they have a hearty bite, so they complement veggies and sauces quite nicely. If you're fit to be tied because you don't have soba noodles, use any other noodle you have on hand. No one will ever know and that's the beauty of homemade meals.

1 lb. boneless pork, cut into 1-inch pieces

1 teaspoon sesame oil

14 oz. bag frozen pre-cut stir-fry vegetables, thawed

1½ cups Asian black bean sauce

½ package soba noodles*, cooked and drained

Pour the oil into the inner pot of the rice cooker and press the Steam/Cook button. Heat the oil and add the pork and sesame oil. Sauté and stir until well-browned. Toss in the vegetables and salt and pepper to taste and give it a quick stir.

Close the lid and cook for 5 to 8 minutes, or until the vegetables are just tender-crisp. Add the black bean sauce and stir to combine. Continue cooking for 5 minutes, or until the sauce is hot and bubbly. Toss the pork and vegetables with the cooked soba noodles and serve hot in bowls.

*WHERE IS IT? Soba noodles are sold fresh, uncooked so you'll usually find them in the produce section of the grocery store next to the wonton wrappers or rice papers, instead of on the pasta/noodle aisle.

chipotle chicken & adobo lime rice

HAVE ON HAND: 1 TBSP EXTRA-VIRGIN OLIVE OIL, SALT & PEPPER | SERVES 4

You're playing with fire with canned chipotle chilies, so tread carefully here. If you're a lightweight, you may want to go with 1 chile to start and 1 tablespoon of sauce from the can. Work your way up from there.

1 lb. boneless, skinless chicken breasts, cut into
    large pieces
2 whole canned chipotle chilies, chopped,
    with 2 tablespoons sauce from can
1½ cups medium-grain white rice, uncooked
3¼ cups chicken broth
Juice of 1 lime

Pour the oil into the inner pot of the rice cooker and press the Steam/Cook button. Heat the oil and add the chicken breasts and chopped chipotles and sauté until lightly browned. Toss in the remaining ingredients and add salt and pepper to taste. Stir well to combine the ingredients.

Close the lid and press the White Rice button. When the cooker switches to the Keep Warm mode, gently fluff the rice with a plastic spatula, close the lid and let stand for a few minutes.

jasmine rice with garbanzos & baby spinach

HAVE ON HAND: 1 TBSP BUTTER, SALT & PEPPER | SERVES 4

This is a one-dish dinner chock full of good-for-you ingredients so it may scare the socks off your family when you serve it. They may even look around longingly for chicken nuggets and French fries to appear, as if by magic. Instead of caving in to the pressure, take a firm grip and serve up this winning entrée with a smile. And, offer some premium fudge ice cream and shortbread cookies for dessert. That'll keep 'em coming back.

1½ cups jasmine rice, uncooked
2½ cups chicken broth
15 oz. can garbanzo beans, drained
15 oz. can diced tomatoes with roasted onion
        and garlic, with juices
2 cups baby spinach leaves, cleaned

Place the butter in the inner pot of the rice cooker and press the Steam/Cook button. Heat the butter and add the rice. Give it a quick stir to coat the grains with butter. Toss in the chicken broth, beans, tomatoes with juices and salt and pepper to taste.

Close the lid and press the White Rice button. When done, open the lid, scatter the spinach on top of the rice, close the lid and continue cooking on the Steam/Cook mode for 10 minutes. Gently fluff the rice, close the lid and let the rice stand for a few remaining minutes.

santa fe pork, rice & bean jumble

HAVE ON HAND: 1 TBSP CANOLA OIL, SALT & PEPPER, 2½ CUPS WATER | SERVES 4

After a day at work that could probably be labeled a "jumble," this big mess of goodness is the perfect conclusion. If you have some sour cream just hanging around, use it to garnish each serving.

1 lb. boneless pork, cut into ½-inch pieces
8 oz. jar tomatillo salsa (or any other salsa)
15 oz. can whole kernel corn, drained
15 oz. can black beans, drained
1½ cups long grain white rice, uncooked

Pour the oil into the inner pot of the rice cooker and press the Steam/Cook button. Heat the oil for 1 minute. Dust the pork with salt and pepper and sauté in the oil until lightly browned, turning the pork occasionally. Toss in the remaining ingredients, add the water and give it all a quick stir.

Close the lid and press the Steam/Cook button. Cook for 25 to 30 minutes and gently fluff the rice. Close the lid and let the rice stand for a few additional minutes.

an easy cheesy chicken

HAVE ON HAND: 1 TBSP BUTTER, SALT & PEPPER | SERVES 4

Perfect for those evenings when the boys are fighting over the TV remote and your daughter is trying to dress the cat in doll clothes.

4 boneless, skinless chicken breasts
15 oz. can diced tomatoes with peppers and
    onions, with juices
1½ cups long grain white rice, uncooked
2½ cups chicken broth
1 cup mozzarella cheese, shredded

Place the butter in the inner pot of the rice cooker and press the Steam/Cook button. Heat the butter and add the chicken breasts. Sauté until lightly browned, turning once. Toss in the remaining ingredients, except the cheese, and add salt and pepper to taste.

Close the lid and Steam/Cook for 30 to 35 minutes or until the chicken is cooked through and the rice is done. Gently fluff the rice, close the lid and let the rice stand for a few minutes. Divide between 4 plates and cover each serving with cheese. (We suggest you find the cat after dinner and serve him a little chicken as well, to soothe his troubled nerves.)

fresh pesto tortellini with balsamic sweet peppers

HAVE ON HAND: SALT & PEPPER | SERVES 4

A little recipe suggestion here...buy some really good Chianti and use it both in the recipe and as your dinner wine. A small jug is good, but a big jug is even better.

1 small jar Italian sweet peppers in balsamic vinegar, or ½ jar sun-dried tomatoes with oil

2 15 oz. cans diced tomatoes with Italian seasoning, with juices

9 ounces refrigerated fresh pesto tortellini, uncooked

¼ cup red wine, or more if needed

½ cup Parmesan cheese, grated

Toss all ingredients, except the Parmesan cheese, into the inner pot of the rice cooker, add salt and pepper to taste and give it a gentle stir to spread the tortellini evenly in the sauce.

Close the lid and Steam/Cook for 14 minutes, opening the lid and gently stirring once or twice. Switch the cooker to Keep Warm mode and let stand for 5 minutes or until the pasta is cooked to your liking. Serve topped with the grated cheese.

marinated artichoke couscous

HAVE ON HAND: SALT & PEPPER | SERVES 4

If you feel especially energetic, grill some chicken breasts to go with this couscous. If you have limited energy, buy rotisserie chicken at the store and serve alongside. If you have zero energy, ignore the chicken completely and serve the couscous as is. It's all good.

1¼ cups chicken broth

6 oz. box plain couscous, uncooked

6.5 oz. jar marinated artichoke hearts, with oil

2 tablespoons jarred eggplant caponata or
    sun-dried tomatoes

Place the broth into the inner pot of the rice cooker and Steam/Cook until it comes to a boil. Toss in all remaining ingredients, add salt and pepper to taste and give it a quick stir. Close the lid and turn off the cooker. Let stand for 5 minutes or until the couscous is tender. Fluff with a fork before serving.

steamed cod with parsley rice pilaf

HAVE ON HAND: 3 TBSP EXTRA-VIRGIN OLIVE OIL, DIVIDED, 1¼ CUPS WATER, SALT & PEPPER | SERVES 4

What to do with cod or any other white, mild fish fillets besides drenching in batter and deep-frying them into high-fat territory? Check out this colorful rice and steamed fillet recipe. Your arteries will love you dearly.

1½ cups white medium-grained rice, uncooked
15 oz. can diced tomatoes with onion and garlic,
    with juices
½ cup fresh parsley leaves, chopped
2 cups fish broth (or vegetable broth)
1 lb. cod fish fillets

Pour 1 tablespoon of the oil into the inner pot of the rice cooker and press the Steam/Cook button. Heat the oil and add the rice. Stir to coat the grains. Toss in the tomatoes and juice, parsley, fish broth, water and salt and pepper to taste and give it a quick stir. Close the lid and Steam/Cook for 22 minutes. Place the cod fillets in the Steam Tray, dust with salt and pepper, open the lid and carefully place the Steam Tray into the cooker. Close the lid and continue to Steam/Cook for 8 to 15 minutes, or until the fish is flaky and the rice is tender.

When the cooker switches to the Keep Warm mode, remove the Steam Tray and cover the fish with foil to keep warm. Fluff the rice, close the lid and let rice stand for a few minutes. Serve the cod over the top of the parsley rice and drizzle with the remaining olive oil.

butternut risotto, oh!

HAVE ON HAND: 2 TBSP EXTRA-VIRGIN OLIVE OIL, 2 TBSP BUTTER, SALT & PEPPER | SERVES 4

Preparing risotto can be a real pain, what with all that slow stirring over low heat and mixing in of the liquids at just the right moment. We say forget it - pop it all into your rice cooker and let nature take its course.

1 small onion, peeled and chopped
1½ cups butternut squash, peeled and cut into
    ½-inch pieces
1 teaspoon dried sage, crumbled
3 cups chicken broth
1 cup Arborio rice, uncooked

Pour the oil into the inner pot of the rice cooker and press the Steam/Cook button. Add the butter and heat with the oil. Add the onions, squash, sage and salt and pepper to taste and sauté until the onions and squash just begin to soften. Add the rice and give it a quick stir to coat the grains. Add 1 cup of broth. Close the lid and Steam/Cook for 8 minutes, opening the lid and stirring now and then. Open the lid and add the remaining chicken broth. Close the lid and continue cooking for 16 to 20 minutes, opening the lid and stirring a few times, until the rice is tender and cooked through.

broccoli couscous with cheddar cheese

HAVE ON HAND: 1¼ CUPS WATER, 1 TBSP EXTRA-VIRGIN OLIVE OIL, SALT & PEPPER | SERVES 4

If you add a few cups of shredded, pre-cooked chicken to this, you'd have a complete meal without even blinking.

2 cups frozen pre-cut broccoli, thawed
6 oz. box roasted garlic and olive oil couscous, uncooked
1 cup cheddar cheese, shredded
¼ cup walnuts, chopped

Place the water and broccoli into the inner pot of the rice cooker and Steam/Cook until it comes to a boil, in about 8 minutes. Toss in the couscous and the flavor packet, add the salt and pepper to taste and give it a quick stir.

Close the lid and turn off the cooker. Let stand for 5 minutes or until the couscous is tender. Open the lid, fluff with a fork and stir in the cheese and walnuts, lightly mixing until the cheese is melted. Serve right away.

a gorgeous mid-week 10 minute bolognese

HAVE ON HAND: 2 TBSP EXTRA-VIRGIN OLIVE OIL, SALT & PEPPER | SERVES 4

Without knowing what kind of busy life you lead, we're taking a wild leap here and assuming you're slammed like the rest of us. Most of us simply pretend to cook during the weeknights, as we hurriedly pull together something that looks like dinner. This valuable little recipe can be an ace in the hole for you on any weeknight – check it out and save it in a secret place because we already know from experience that you're going to love it.

¾ lb. lean ground beef
24-oz. jar tomato mushroom spaghetti sauce
12 oz. package fresh linguine noodles, cut in half
1 cup Chianti wine
1 cup Parmesan cheese, grated

Pour the oil into the inner pot of the rice cooker and press the Steam/Cook button. Heat the oil and add the beef. Sauté until well-browned. Add the spaghetti sauce and wine and Steam/Cook for 5 minutes, or until the sauce starts to bubble. Add the salt and pepper to taste and toss in the pasta, separating the noodles as you drop them in. Give it a good stir to ensure the strands are separated.

Close the lid and Steam/Cook for 15 minutes, opening the lid and stirring occasionally to prevent the noodles from sticking together. Add additional red wine or water if the sauce becomes too thick.

Switch the cooker to Keep Warm mode and allow the Bolognese to stay warm for 2 to 6 minutes, or until the pasta is done to your liking. Serve with generous amounts of the grated cheese.

savory artichoke garlic chicken with winter squash pilaf

HAVE ON HAND: 2 TBSP BUTTER, SALT & PEPPER | SERVES 4

Somebody with brains (and now lots of money) dreamt up the chicken-plus-gourmet-ingredients-sausage idea. If you can't find this flavored sausage, grab any other variety that sounds good to you and go for it.

1½ cups mixed long-grain brown and wild rice, uncooked
3¼ cups chicken broth
1½ tablespoon dried sage
1 lb. package pre-cooked artichoke garlic chicken sausage, cut into 1-inch pieces
1 large butternut squash, peeled and cut into 1-inch pieces

Place the butter in the inner pot of the rice cooker and press the Steam/Cook button. Heat the butter and add the rice; sauté for a few minutes to coat the grains. Toss in the chicken broth and sage, close the lid and press the Brown Rice button.

After the rice cooks for 60 minutes, open the lid and toss in the squash and sausage; do not stir. Close the lid and continue cooking. When the cooker switches to the Keep Warm mode, give the rice a quick stir, close the lid and let stand for a few minutes. Toss with additional butter, if desired.

penne pasta with homemade vodka sauce

HAVE ON HAND: 2 CUPS WATER | SERVES 4

Vodka? Did someone say "vodka?" We're all about this cheesy, creamy vodka sauce, thanks to several volunteers who stepped up for heavy-duty taste-testing during the creation of this recipe, all for the betterment of mankind and world peace.

24-oz. jar smooth marinara sauce

¾ cup good-quality vodka

4 oz. package cream cheese, softened and cut
    into small pieces

6 ounces penne pasta, uncooked

½ cup Parmesan cheese, grated

Pour the marinara sauce and vodka into the inner pot of the rice cooker and whisk in the cream cheese. Add the water and give it a good stir to combine. Add the pasta and stir again. Close the lid and Steam/Cook for about 25 minutes, opening the lid and stirring frequently to prevent the pasta from sticking together. Add additional vodka or water if the sauce becomes too thick. Serve with the grated cheese.

quick cooking barley risotto with arugula & sun-dried tomatoes

HAVE ON HAND: 2 CUPS WATER, SALT & PEPPER | SERVES 4

Arugula is mysterious. A second cousin shirt-tail relative of the mustard family, arugula is also called "rocket" in certain countries. Must be similar to a rutabaga, which is also known as "swede" in various places. We're flummoxed.

½ cup oil packed sun-dried tomatoes, chopped,
       plus 2 tablespoons of the oil
2 cups quick-cooking barley
⅔ cup dry white wine
2¾ cups chicken broth
2 cups wild arugula, chopped

Pour 1 tablespoon of the sun-dried tomato oil into the inner pot of the rice cooker. Press the Steam/Cook button and heat the oil. Add the barley and sauté until the barley becomes fragrant and begins to toast, about 3 minutes. Add the wine and give it a quick stir.

Add the chicken broth, sun-dried tomatoes with the remaining oil, water and salt and pepper to taste. Close the lid and continue cooking for 10 minutes, stirring frequently. Toss in the arugula and Steam/Cook for an additional 10 minutes.

When the cooker switches to the Keep Warm mode, give the barley a quick stir, close the lid and let it stand for a few minutes, or until the barley is tender. If you have Parmesan cheese on hand, go ahead and stir some into the risotto.

garlic basil linguine with pesto alfredo sauce

HAVE ON HAND: 2 CUPS WATER, SALT & PEPPER | SERVES 4

Big flavors building here...add a salad and a loaf of crusty bread and you're home free!

16 oz. jar Alfredo sauce
2 tablespoons jarred pesto, or more to taste
4 ounces dried garlic basil linguine*, uncooked
½ cup Parmesan cheese, grated
¼ cup fresh parsley, chopped

Toss all ingredients, except the grated cheese, into the inner pot of the rice cooker and stir well. Add 2 cups of water and stir to blend again.

Close the lid and Steam/Cook for about 15 to 20 minutes, opening the lid and stirring frequently to prevent the pasta strands from sticking together. Add additional water if the sauce becomes too thick. Serve with a sprinkling of parsley and a smattering of grated Parmesan cheese.

*WHERE IS IT? You can find all kinds of flavored pastas – spinach, sun-dried tomato, etc. etc. in the pasta aisle at the grocery store. For a fun twist, we sometimes check out the kosher aisle to find delicious specialty pasta.

mediterranean lamb with gigantes butter beans

HAVE ON HAND: ½ CUP EXTRA-VIRGIN OLIVE OIL, DIVIDED, SALT & PEPPER | SERVES 4

We think lamb deserves more attention for two important reasons: First, because one of us is Greek and loves lamb accordingly, and second, because it is so distinctly flavorful, but most folks don't know enough about lamb to prepare it correctly. Oh, woe is to me if you don't try this recipe and agree with us!

2 tablespoons tomato paste

¾ lb. boneless lamb, cut into 1-inch pieces

2 15 oz. cans giant butter beans or white beans, drained

15 oz. can diced tomatoes with onion and green bell pepper, with juices

2 teaspoons ground Greek seasoning*

Pour 2 tablespoons of the oil into the inner pot of the rice cooker and press the Steam/Cook button. Heat the oil for a couple of minutes. Dust the lamb with salt and pepper and sauté in the oil until well browned, turning occasionally. Add the remaining ingredients, except the remaining olive oil, and give it a quick stir.

Close the lid and Steam/Cook for 8 minutes, opening the lid and stirring frequently, but gently, until the lamb is done and the beans are hot through. Transfer to a serving bowl and drizzle with the remaining olive oil.

*WHERE IS IT? Greek seasoning is a blend of exotic spices and you'll find it in the spice aisle. Use it in salad dressings, egg dishes, yogurt-based sauces and wherever you think it works.

pesto chicken sausage with lentils & arugula

HAVE ON HAND: 1 TBSP EXTRA-VIRGIN OLIVE OIL, SALT & PEPPER | SERVES 4

Sure, you could cook your own lentils and make your own sausage, but, really…why?

1 lb. pre-cooked pesto chicken sausage, cut into
    1-inch pieces
1 small carton French onion soup
10 oz. package pre-cooked lentils*
2 cups arugula, rinsed and drained
½ cup Gruyere cheese, grated

Pour the oil into the inner pot of the rice cooker and press the Steam/Cook button. Heat the oil and add the sausage. Cook and sauté until browned. Add a small amount of the soup and use a plastic spatula to make sure any browned bits are removed from the bottom of the pot. Add the remaining soup and lentils, give it a quick stir, close the lid and Steam/Cook for 10 to 12 minutes, stirring occasionally. Open the lid, toss in the arugula, sprinkle with salt and pepper, and Steam/Cook just until the arugula has wilted. Serve topped with the grated cheese.

*WHERE IS IT? This one's a little tricky, so your best bet is to ask a clerk for help if you can't find pre-cooked lentils. And, it's okay to ask. One of us has a husband who didn't know the difference between a cucumber and a zucchini and refused to ask, precipitating a big cooking emergency, but you probably don't want to hear that story…

risi e pisi, pleasi! (rice with peas, please)

HAVE ON HAND: 2 TBSP EXTRA-VIRGIN OLIVE OIL, 2 TBSP BUTTER, SALT & PEPPER | SERVES 4

The only authentic way to prepare this recipe is by singing the recipe title over and over as you prep the food. For best results, make up your own musical score to accompany these lyrics and bust a couple of moves while you continue prepping.

1 medium onion, peeled and chopped
1 cup Arborio rice, uncooked
1 cup dry white wine
2 cups chicken broth
1 cup frozen peas, thawed

Pour the oil into the inner pot of the rice cooker and press the Steam/Cook button. Heat the oil and add the onions, salt and pepper to taste. Stir and sauté until softened. Toss in the rice and stir to coat the grains. Add the wine, close the lid and Steam/Cook for 8 minutes, opening the lid and stirring frequently to prevent sticking. Add the chicken broth, close the lid and continue cooking for 16 to 20 minutes, opening the lid and stirring frequently, until the rice is tender and cooked through. Add the peas just before the end of the cooking time, stirring until the peas are warmed.

wine-poached pears with caramel

HAVE ON HAND: PINCH OF SALT | SERVES 4

Sweet, warm fruit imbued with a subtle wine flavor and rich caramel sauce. Oh, and, by the way, almost no prep work. Count me in!

2 cups sweet dessert wine
½ teaspoon ground nutmeg
2 large pears, halved and cored
¼ cup premium caramel sauce
Whipped cream for garnish

Pour the wine into the inner pot of the rice cooker and add the nutmeg. Place the pears, cut side down, in the wine. Steam/Cook for 12 minutes, or until the pears are tender. Place half of a pear on each dessert plate and drizzle with the caramel sauce. Toss a dollop of whipped cream over each serving if you're feeling especially generous.

sweet maple apple rice pudding

HAVE ON HAND: 2 TBSP BUTTER, 1 CUP WATER, ⅓ CUP BROWN SUGAR, OR MORE TO TASTE | SERVES 4

When it is 101 degrees in the shade and you can't take it anymore....hide!! Rent a few wintry movies, turn the air conditioner down to a chilly 65 degrees, put on your warmest slippers and throw together a classic comfort food...rice pudding. We guarantee you'll forget how hot it is outside. Don't forget the hot cocoa.

1 cup Arborio rice, uncooked
1 cup apple juice
1 cup chunky applesauce
1 cup lowfat milk
3 tablespoons maple syrup

Place the butter in the inner pot of the rice cooker and press the Steam/Cook button. Toss in the rice and apple juice and, with the lid open, cook and stir frequently until the juice is absorbed, about 8 minutes. Add the applesauce, milk and water and give it a good stir to combine.

Close the lid and Steam/Cook for 20 minutes, opening the lid and stirring frequently until the rice is tender. When the rice cooker switches to the Keep Warm mode, stir in the maple syrup and brown sugar and let the pudding stand for 5 minutes.

delish in a dish, sweet chocolate rice pudding

SERVES 4

With such a sweet way to use leftover rice, you will no doubt start planning rice dinners all week. Change up the flavors to create your family's new favorite desserts. Add butterscotch topping and white chocolate chips or fresh fruit and almonds........Oh, just save yourself some trouble and make a double batch of rice right now.

2 tablespoons cocoa powder
1 cup canned evaporated milk
1 cup canned sweetened condensed milk
3 cups cooked and cooled medium-grained
    white rice
½ cup semi-sweet chocolate chips

In a medium bowl, mix the cocoa powder with 2 tablespoons evaporated milk until well-blended. Add the rest of the evaporated milk and the condensed milk and whisk to combine. Toss the cooked rice into the inner pot of the rice cooker, add the milk mixture and give it a quick stir.

Close the lid, press the Steam/Cook button and cook for 10 minutes, or until it reaches the desired consistency. Stir in the chocolate chips, give it a quick stir and serve the pudding while warm.

thai ginger's world famous coconut rice pudding

SERVES 4

Thai Ginger was a notorious red-headed pirate. She sailed with a rowdy lot and a tough life it t'was for ole Ginger, with women's lib near' five or six centuries away. She was forced to walk the plank off a remote Caribbean island. Lucky girl washed up on shore where the locals, who had never seen red hair, thought she was a god. She passed the time by perfecting the island's favorite rice pudding recipe and when she was rescued by the Red Coats and hustled back to England, she made a fortune selling her famous pudding. The motto of this story is…when life hands you coconuts, turn'em into pudding.

1 cup coconut milk
1 cup sweetened condensed milk
½ teaspoon ground ginger
½ cup pineapple chunks
3 cups cooked and cool medium-grained white rice

Toss all ingredients into the inner pot of the rice cooker and give it a good stir to combine. Close the lid, press the Steam/Cook button and let the rice pudding cook for about 15 to 20 minutes, or until it reaches the desired consistency. Stir often. Serve the pudding while warm.

pumpkin pie dessert risotto

HAVE ON HAND: 2 TBSP BUTTER, 1 CUP WATER, ⅓ CUP BROWN SUGAR, OR MORE TO TASTE | SERVES 4

If Thanksgiving was celebrated in Italy, this perfectly balanced risotto would most likely be served as dessert. Sweet pumpkin and tangy apples dance together to create a rich and creamy risotto pudding. Don't let on about the lowfat milk and very little sugar and no one will ever guess this scrumptious dessert is actually a very healthy choice. Ciao Bella!

1 small yellow apple, peeled and chopped
3 cups cooked and cooled medium-grain
    white rice
1 cup apple juice
16 oz. can pumpkin pie filling
1 cup lowfat milk

Place the butter in the inner pot of the rice cooker and press the Steam/Cook button. Heat the butter and add the apple. Stir and sauté until just softened. Add the rice and apple juice and, with the lid open, cook, stirring frequently, until the juice is absorbed, about 8 minutes. Add the pumpkin, milk and water and give it a good stir to combine.

Close the lid and Steam/Cook for 20 minutes, opening the lid and stirring frequently until the rice is tender. When the rice cooker switches to the Keep Warm mode, let the pudding stand for 5 minutes. Open the lid and add the brown sugar to taste.

lavish southern belle spoon bread

HAVE ON HAND: 2 CUPS WATER, ⅓ CUP MAYONNAISE, COOKING SPRAY | SERVES 4 TO 6

When plebian corn bread just won't do, haul out this recipe for decadent and rich Southern spoon bread. Packed with Swiss cheese, cream cheese, sour cream and creamed corn, it's enough to make a Southern belle swoon.

1 large egg, beaten
1 cup Jiffy™ corn muffin mix
¾ cup canned creamed corn
¾ cup sour cream
¾ cup Swiss cheese, shredded

Completely line the Steam Tray of the rice cooker with 2 large pieces of aluminum foil to create a spill-proof liner and lightly coat with cooking spray. In a mixing bowl, combine the egg, corn muffin mix, creamed corn, sour cream and Swiss cheese and give it all a good stir. Add the mayonnaise and stir to blend. Pour the water into the inner pot and position the Steam Tray in the cooker. Spoon the cornbread mixture into the prepared Steam Tray and Steam/Cook for 30 to 35 minutes, or until the cornbread is very moist, almost pudding-like, but set in the middle. Remove the Steam Tray from the cooker and cool slightly on a wire rack. Spoon into bowls and top with other yummy garnishes such as butter or honey if you feel like it. We'll never tell.

old fashioned bread pudding

HAVE ON HAND: 2½ CUPS WATER, 3 TBSP SUGAR, 2 TBSP BUTTER, ½ TSP GROUND NUTMEG | SERVES 2

This is the dessert that grandmothers served on Sundays after their famous fried chicken family dinner. It turns grumpy people happy, rainy days into sunshine, frogs into princes, and all with just five ingredients. We want to be honest, so we have to say this dessert will take more than 5 minutes to prep. We couldn't bear to exclude it from this book, so forgive us for this indulgence. After you taste this, we think you'll appreciate the indulgence, too.

1 large egg
¼ teaspoon vanilla extract
⅔ cup whole milk
1 cup stale French bread, cut into ½ inch cubes
¼ cup raisins

Use 1 tablespoon of softened butter to generously butter the inside of 2 heatproof coffee mugs. (Make sure the mugs will safely fit into the inner pot of the rice cooker.) Pour the water into the inner pot, close the lid, press the Steam/Cook button and bring the water to a boil.

In a medium bowl, whisk together the eggs and sugar until well-blended. Add the vanilla, milk and nutmeg and give it a good whisk to thoroughly combine. Melt 1 tablespoon of butter in the microwave and add to the bowl, stirring well to blend. Divide the bread cubes between the 2 prepared mugs and scatter the raisins over the top. Divide the egg mixture between the 2 mugs, filling each no more than two-thirds full. Cover each mug tightly with foil.

Using an oversized oven mitt, carefully place the mugs into the boiling water in the inner pot. Close the lid and cook for 25 to 30 minutes, or until a knife inserted into the center of each mug comes out clean. When done, carefully lift out the mugs, cool slightly and serve warm.

chocolate chocolate chip clouds

HAVE ON HAND: 2 TBSP SOFTENED BUTTER, 2½ CUPS WATER, ½ CUP FLOUR, ¼ CUP SUGAR | SERVES 2

Dark clouds don't always bring frowns...especially these light-as-a-feather chocolate cakes. Baked in their own serving mug, just plop a scoop of vanilla bean ice cream on top and forgo the fighting over who got the biggest piece.....another reason to smile.

2 tablespoons powdered unsweetened
     baking cocoa
¼ teaspoon baking powder
1 egg
¼ cup whole milk
½ cup semi-sweet chocolate chips

Use 1 tablespoon of softened butter to generously butter the inside of 2 heatproof coffee mugs. (Make sure the mugs will safely fit inside the inner pot of the rice cooker). Pour the water into the inner pot, close the lid, press the Steam/Cook button and bring the water to a boil.

In a small bowl, mix the flour, cocoa powder and baking powder until completely combined and set aside. In a medium bowl, use the back of a tablespoon to smoosh together the remaining butter with the sugar, until very well-blended. Whisk the egg into the butter and sugar mixture and blend until well-combined. Add a little of the flour/cocoa mixture and blend, then add a little milk and blend, continuing mixing well after each addition, until all the milk and flour are added. Stir in the chocolate chips.

Divide the batter between the 2 prepared mugs. Cover each mug tightly with foil. Using an oversized oven mitt, place the mugs into the boiling water. Close the lid and cook for 25 minutes, or until a knife inserted into the center comes out clean.

When done, lift the mugs to a wire rack to cool. Serve the cakes in the mugs or run a knife around the edge and pop the cakes out onto plates or into bowls.

tea time in a mug, english soda cake with raisins

HAVE ON HAND: 1 TBSP BUTTER, SOFTENED, 2 CUPS WATER, ¼ CUP HOT WATER, ¾ CUPS FLOUR | SERVES 2

The addition of a caramel sauce is just the ticket to compliment a not too sweet English cake. As with scones, the taste of the soda is evident, hence it's name. Raisins give the very famous English pudding, Spotted Dog, its name. I guess we could call this....Spot o' Tea Soda Cake.

¼ cup light corn syrup
1 teaspoon baking soda
½ teaspoon ground allspice
½ cup raisins
¼ cup caramel sauce

Generously butter the inside of 2 heatproof coffee mugs. (Make sure that the mugs safely fit inside the inner pot of the rice cooker.) Pour 2 cups of water into the inner pot, close the lid and press the Steam/Cook button. Bring the water to a boil in about 8 minutes.

In a medium mixing bowl, blend the ¼ cup hot water with the corn syrup in a mixing bowl. Add the soda, allspice, flour and raisins and blend until well-combined.

Spoon the batter into the prepared coffee mugs, filling them no more than two-thirds of the way full. Cover each mug tightly with foil and, using an oversized oven mitt, place the mugs into the inner pot, close the lid and press the Steam/Cook button. Cook for 30 to 40 minutes.

Test for doneness after 30 minutes; the cake should be firm and spongy. When done, use oversized oven mitts to remove the mugs from the cooker. Serve warm in mugs or run a knife around the edge and pop the soda cakes out onto a rack to cool. Drizzle the caramel sauce over each warm serving.

fresh summer fruit shortcake

HAVE ON HAND: 2 CUPS SUGAR, 1 CUP WATER | SERVES 6

When you've put away the snow shovel and the lake is calling your name, you know it's time for summer shortcake. Hit the farmers market and scoop up all the fresh fruit you (or your teenagers) can carry and hurry home to make this luscious dessert.

1 lb. fresh peaches, peeled and sliced
1 lb. apricots, peeled and sliced
1 lb. cherries, stemmed and seeded
1 purchased pound cake, thickly sliced
1 container prepared whipped cream

Toss the sugar and water into the inner pot of the rice cooker and give it a quick stir. Close the lid, press the Steam/Cook button and cook for 5 minutes to make a sugar syrup. Add the fruit, stir well, and cook until the fruit is tender, about 8 to 10 minutes. Serve the hot fruit and syrup over a slice of pound cake and top with the whipped cream.

medieval happy hour mulled apple cider

HAVE ON HAND: BUTTER, IF DESIRED | SERVES 8

Being a Medieval knight wasn't easy, with all the jousting and conquering in ill-fitting tights and smelly old armor. And the chafing...don't get us started! So, if anyone deserved a friendly game of darts and a toothless smile from a serving wench, it was he. Ditching the heavy iron zoot suit gave happy hour a whole new meaning.

½ gallon apple cider or apple juice
¼ cup brown sugar
½ oz. mulling spices*
8 shots brandy
8 cinnamon sticks

Pour the apple cider, brown sugar and mulling spices into the inner pot of the rice cooker and give it a quick stir. Close the lid, press the Steam/Cook button and cook for 8 to 10 minutes. When the cooker switches to the Keep Warm mode, let the mulled cider stand for about 10 minutes. Serve in tall glass mugs with a spoonful of butter, a shot of brandy and a cinnamon stick.

 *WHERE IS IT? Mulling spices are easily found in the spice aisle and once you buy some, take one whiff of the aroma, and you'll find a wealth of reasons to use this aromatic medley.

caramel coco chanel

HAVE ON HAND: ¼ CUP WATER | SERVES 4

It's rumored that this decadent drink was Coco's beverage of choice after a hectic designing frenzy in her famous Paris studio. Chanel put forth the view that women should dress for themselves and not for their men...so, in that spirit, make this charming cup of independence for yourself...and share some with the rest of your family.

⅓ cup sugar
⅓ cup unsweetened cocoa powder
2 tablespoons premium caramel topping
4 cups whole milk
2 cups half and half cream

Toss the sugar, cocoa and water into the inner pot of the rice cooker. Press the Steam/Cook button and cook, stirring constantly to dissolve the sugar, for about 3 minutes. Add the caramel and give it a good stir to combine. Stir in the milk and cream and blend again. Close the cover and cook for 5 minutes or until the cocoa is hot.

index